Alan Osborne was b[illegible]
1942 and educated at Quak[illegible]
He boxed and swam comp[illegible]
Youth Standard before stud[illegible]
Art.

His early career was devoted to education, he taught art and architecture in Oxford and London where he was involved in developing the Design and Technology Syllabus. He returned to Wales in 1975 to teach at Afon Taf, Troed-y-Rhiw.

His dramatic work began with *Plans for The Great Trapeze Act* and was followed by *Terraces*, *Johnny Darkie* and his first major work *Bull, Rock and Nut* which won the Play for Wales competition in 1981 and began his long association with The Made In Wales Stage company. *In Sunshine and In Shadow* followed in 1985 with performances in Wales and London. *Redemption Song*, the final play in *The Merthyr Trilogy* being performed in 1987. He has also written a number of successful television dramas including *The Whistling Boy (1994)* and *The Beach Inspector (1996)*. A full retrospective of his work was staged by Made In Wales and performed at the Sherman Theatre in 1993.

He has composed music scores to many of his plays and *Give us the Flowers Now* for the BBC Symphony Orchestra and a choral libretto, *Spirit of Our Distant Fathers in Wales* which toured with Brecon High School in the United States.

His art work has also received numerous exhibitions and is held in many private and public collections.

He lives in Cardiff.

The Merthyr Trilogy

Three Plays

Alan Osborne

PARTHIAN BOOKS

Parthian
The Old Surgery
Napier Street
Cardigan
SA43 1ED
www.parthianbooks.co.uk

First Published in 1998
Reprinted 2005

Edited by Gilly Adams and Arranged by Dorien Thomas

ISBN 0952155869

Printed and bound by Lightning Source

Parthian is an independent publisher that works with the financial support of the Welsh Books Council

A cataloguing record for this book is available from the British Library

Cover Design: Lucy Llewellyn

Cover photography: Photolibrary Wales

For Dorien Thomas,
solver of problems with
insight
and energy.

Contents

Give us the Flowers Now

More than twenty years of regular theatre going in Wales produces a kind of flotsam in the memory. Images and words drift to the surface of the mind. Sometimes it is possible to identify them with titles and a context. On other occasions the mental picture eludes categorisation. Amongst these fragments from my past, Alan Osborne's Merthyr plays reach me in comparatively clear definition, partly because of my intense involvement with them, but also because of their inherent power. As a requiem for the urban poor, of South Wales and the World, they remain unequalled.

I knew Alan's work from his operas *Terraces* and *Johnny Darkie,* both of which explored the lives of different communities, the Valleys and Tiger Bay respectively, through cycles of poems and songs, for which Alan wrote the words and the music. My more intimate involvement with his theatre writing began with the Play for Wales Competition in 1981. This was organised by Sue Harries at the Welsh Academy and I was invited, as the then Drama Director of the Welsh Arts Council, to help sift through the scripts before handing on the plays worthy of short listing to the more illustrious judges. In the event this was a more difficult task than we'd anticipated because the competition seemed to have caused a great clearing out of cupboards, resulting in a dusty and lack lustre set of entries Amongst them was a fragment, written phonetically in the particular idiom of the Valleys. Bursting with energy, incoherent, unfinished, it was nevertheless a theatre piece about real people written by someone who understood what made his characters tick and with a gift of language. This turned out to be the first draft of *Bull, Rock and Nut.*

Two years later, through a development process of rehearsed readings and workshops, the play was premiered by the Made in Wales Stage Company at the Bethesda Arts Centre, Merthyr Tydfil in the Autumn of 1983. By that time I'd extricated myself from the Welsh Arts Council and was working part-time as a kind of Literary Manager or Project Director for Made in Wales, work which was to take over the next decade of my life as I eventually became the Artistic Director - but that's another story.

Bull, Rock and Nut was an immensely important play. Set in a cafe in Merthyr on the day of Johnny Owen's funeral, the play took up themes which have concerned Alan ever since -- the break down of community, the desperation of lives without hope, the power of (male) friendship -- and expressed them through a poetic language, at once obscene, funny, pathetic, and vital. The essence of the play is summed up in the impassioned speech which Nut (*"I got the words, (Rock) got the songs, (Bull) got the muscles."*) makes to the cafe owner whom he perceives as indifferent

"Here's the tragedy, Luigi. In here. Gives us the flowers now, Luigi. Give us the flowers now! This is the new war, jobless, hopeless, pissy! Dead soldiers stuck together, slit smiles like dead sheep. Gives us the flowers now! When we can still smell 'em.."

There is no doubt in my mind that *Bull, Rock and Nut* was a bench mark. It moved theatre in Wales forward because it dealt with contemporary issues in language which was transformative.

Hugh Thomas' production was graced with definitive performances from Roger Nott, Terry Jackson and Dorien Thomas as the eponymous trio, actors whose own history allowed them to identify with the characters they were playing. There was a kind of savage humour in the exchanges between the men, with a lot of word play and rhyming slang of a particular Valleys' idiom, allied with a wild physicality, which simply had not been put on stage before. On a more practical level, the other particular memory of that production was that the set was stolen early on in the tour, and only the empty van was recovered, leaving a difficult insurance negotiation about the elaborately authentic Espresso machine which had been borrowed for the show.

Two years later, in April 1985, Made in Wales mounted its first Write On! Festival, which was a real triumph of mind over matter, with a small company of actors performing six plays and giving rehearsed readings of six more, and all in the space of ten days. I had had difficulty in finding a play for the last night of the festival and the publicity brochure pragmatically promised 'Mystery Guest Time'. Somewhere along the line Alan came to the rescue with *In Sunshine and In Shadow* and it was this play which became both the culmination and the hit of that Write On! Strangely, given the lack of advance publicity, enough people appeared to fill the Sherman Arena and there was a sense of occasion, of something significant taking place, as well as a kind of shock wave at the bleakness and brutality of what was being depicted under the black humour. The play deals with child abuse and drug abuse in the context of extreme poverty. This extraordinary portrait of the monstrous and pathetic Vee, who yearns to be a singer and lives in a haze of day dreams and drugs, simultaneously loving and loathing her children, the hapless Babes and the autistic Ga-Ga, was at once hilariously funny and savage in its indictment of a society wholly indifferent to the desperation of the deprived. Its impact on the audience was gut-wrenching and there were tears amid the laughter.

A full production of *In Sunshine* toured Wales later that year and later again it was taken up by another Welsh company, Merthyr Inc. and performed at the Battersea Arts Centre. Interestingly, eight years after its first reading, the play featured as the high-light of the Write On ! 1993 festival, which as well as exploring entirely new work, presented a retrospective of Alan's work. On this occasion I was able to fulfil a long held ambition to direct *In Sunshine.* It was clear, both in rehearsals, and from the audience response, that the play had not dated or lost any of its original impact. If anything, fourteen years of Thatcherism had increased the relevance of the drama and made it even more harrowing. The characters had become almost archetypal, in particular Babes, "*the dullest girl in Wales*" with the saucepan jammed on her head, and Cissie the dignified and witty valleys homosexual, whose rape by Stack and Bernie is the rape of the Artist by society. Working on the play, it seemed to me that the emphasis had shifted somehow and there was more ambiguity, so that it was possible to play with the lack of demarcation between the inner and outer worlds of the characters. We were able to question whether Vee ever left the room or whether the more surreal elements of her story took place in some kind of dreamscape. This room for manoeuvre within the text was an indication of the strength and durability of the writing. However interpreted, *In Sunshine and In Shadow* was confirmed as a hugely important play.

The Redemption Song also reappeared in the 1993 retrospective, having first been performed in Write on! 87. Again, this is a heart breaking vision of men who have nothing. Mick has invented a toy which might make his fortune, but he and his mate Bob are dope-heads and we know they will never "*take the toy to Swansea.*", and that even if Bo Bo and Bunny don't get them, someone else will. Underneath the hallucinatory world of the play in which the heavies ease in and out of the action in an increasingly surreal way, there is the profound sadness of the failure of Mick's relationship with Sharon. The workshop production in 1987 focused on the dreamy, dope induced atmosphere out of which the nightmare emerged. The performance in '93 put much more emphasis on the hopeless humour and the strange exuberance of the exchanges between the men. Both productions revelled in the rhythms and cadences of the language.

All the plays in *The Merthyr Trilogy* inhabit a twilight world where people live on an edge between fantasy and reality. "*Give me nothing and I'll be nothing*" says Nut and this is true in some sense for all the protagonists. Each of them confronts the abyss and some of them don't come out alive. The artist is an outsider who attempts to make a mark but can hardly survive. It is a bleak world, but it is enlivened by poetry and rhetoric, by dark humour and friendship and, above all, by an energy which somehow celebrates these desperate lives.

In the ten years since Alan Osborne wrote these plays other writers have emerged with similar preoccupations and a feel for the rich poetic idiom of English speaking, urban South Wales but Alan was the first. He can be said to have pioneered a genre of dramatic writing and, whilst other writers have had more acclaim, it would be my contention that these plays remain unsurpassed. Now that the plays exist in print I hope they will reach the wider audience that they deserve and be seen not just as history, but as living texts of continuing relevance to anyone who cares about theatre.

Gilly Adams,
1998

In rehearsal. Photo: Ian Lawrence

BULL, ROCK, AND NUT

Bull, Rock and Nut was premiéred by Made in Wales Stage Company at the Bethesda Arts Centre, Merthyr Tydfil in October 1983 with the following cast.

BULL: *Ex-fighter* Roger Nott
ROCK: *Ex-fighter* Terry Jackson
NUT: *Their Manager* Dorien Thomas
LUIGI: *Cafe Owner* Robert Blythe
JACKY SIMS: *Manager* Ray Handy
BILLY FLOWERS: *Fighter* Tony Etoria

directed by **Hugh Thomas**
designed by **Simon Banham**
sound & lighting **Peter Zygadlo**
project director **Gilly Adams**

Italian Cafe, Merthyr. The morning of Johnny Owen's funeral. A large silver espresso coffee machine dominates the counter. Sweet jars and sweet trays are laid in a display on the counter. Behind the counter some brown shelves hold a variety of tobaccos and cigarettes and chocolate boxes. In the window are trays of cakes and pastries with a few fluffy toys. Across the window in a semi-circle are large imposing letters: 'Little Roma Cafe'. Each table has four wooden chairs. On the surface of each table there are green ceramic tiles. There is an open door to the left of the service counter. Through the door is a room, dark and old: in need of renovation. A crucifix hangs on the wall. Two naked electric light bulbs hang down. Luigi, the cafe owner, is sixty with thick grey hair and a dark grey moustache. Stalinesque. A collarless shirt buttoned to the neck. He is tidying shelves and cleaning with a rag. Luigi talks to a solitary figure sitting at a table. The solitary figure is big and broad, and wears his long straggling hair in a classic lead guitar style of the nineteen sixties.

Luigi Day shud all der pubs today mun. *Accent of Italian Welsh/Brooklyn.* Day shud all der pubs today mun. You know dat? Hey, Bull, all der pubs shud dill doo o'glog.... *silence* You wanna drink? I give you shandy den. Nod all dat strong, good God.... bedder than nuttin.

Bull *Turns his head slowly and glares at Luigi. Taps his lips with his fingers, continuously.* Too much.... too much of this, you got. Too much of this bastard mouth. Right? Too much bastard mouth. *Changes the tapping, taps his forehead.* See this? Sooner or later you'll get this. Right? The head will sort you out, bastard mouth.

Luigi *Used to such responses, with expert tact.* Right oh den. You wan asprin? Where you go last night, uh? *Bull turns his head and smiles, susceptible to all kinds of flattery, even slander. Luigi laughs.* You awful boy, Bull, uh. You fight lass night?

Bull Broke his mouth, right. They'll have to wire his puss. *Staring at Luigi* Know Benny Jumper? Know him? They calls him muscles. Know him? He had this *taps his head* and this *taps his fist* and this *points to his knee.* He knows, right? Now he knows who's King. Who's the King, Luigi bastard mouth?

Luigi You, Bull, you always King, I know, always.

Bull *Staring, quietly in a friendly tone.* Have I give you a 'ammering yet, bastard mouth?

Luigi Yeah, sure, twice Bull. Tree times I think.. Tree times.

Bull *Pointing to his own lips.* Well, learn to shut this then.

Luigi *Tactfully.* He's a good boy den, dis boy who died. Dey say you'd be greader fighter years ago. Uh? Bull? Bull? Hey Bull. Woss yew guards, Bull? How you spar up, uh?

Bull *Stares in space. Suddenly stands and poses and dances, shadow boxing an imaginary foe. Exhausted, he stops, hands on the counter and butts it with his forehead.* You dun understand, right!

Luigi *Cleaning a cup and watching, quickly responds.* Good fighter, good bogser you are Bull. You could have bin really grade.

Bull dances away, flashing his fists into the air. Luigi smiles to himself and continues wiping the counter. The crowds are gathering outside the cafe window. Voices are heard. They wait for the hero's funeral cortege. Luigi finds a mistake in the old till. Continually, he presses a hammer. Ching. Ching. Ching. Bull stands punching the air. A man enters. He is dressed in a white mackintosh and black tan, and he wears dark glasses. He stands watching Bull's performance.

Nut *Claps his hands and shouts in mock affected effeminate tones.* Well, well, well. Look at our lovely big bear dancing. Ladies and gentlemen! I give you Bull! Your favourite dancing star. Straight out of the Billy Blood and Sybil Flesh School of Dancing. *Nut turns to Luigi and changes his tone.* You encourage this, Luigi Pasteroni Pomeroni del Poof? *Luigi turns, dismissing Nut with a wave of the hand, and continues hammering the till. Nut walks up to Bull's back. Bull is jigging and belting the imaginary. He moves into Bull's guard, into a two person tango position, and holds Bull's clenched fists.* Let's dance, you violent toy, you!

Bull Get off, Nut. Nut, you're a nut. Get off, Nut, I'm winning. *The dance humour possesses sufficient serum to counter balance Bull's wild performance. Bull laughs.* Nut! You're a nut. You're a nut, Nut!

Nut Tea and toast, Luigi the Gee-Gee.

Bull *Holds out his fist.* It don't mean you don't get this, right?

Nut What do you want that for, darling? I've got my own.

Bull *Laughs.* See, you're a nut, Nut! *Picks up Nut and carries him to the green tiled table. They sit laughing. Luigi brings over the food. Bull traps Luigi's hand.* I hate you this morning.

Luigi See, look at your hand. It loog real champ's hand. You shoulda finished yewer bogsing garreer.

Bull *Stands sharply. Emotional and incomprehensible speech, punch-drunk.* Right. O.K. This boy is dead, right. Real champ. Am I right? Real champion. And they said to me, here you are. Money right. *To Nut* 'Member the fella who spits with the big car? We'll be behind you, right? And he's dead out there. A real champ. Gone in a bastard box. In a bastard box.

Bull stands in a punch-drunk haze. Luigi walks away, scratching his head.

Nut *Stands, holds Bull's shoulders.* Oi! Oi! Did I tell you about the man who invented aspirins? Died of a headache.

Bull *Laughs, and with a sudden seriousness, Capone makes a speech* Anyone...anyone who touches you, Nut, will have to see me. You'll be O.K.with me Nut.
A holy silence.

Nut Luigi! What time are the pubs open?

Luigi Doo o'clock. Than Godt!

Nut Time now, Luigi.

Luigi Issa ten to one. *Leaning over the counter and wiping cutlery* Whad I dun understand iss why you all stay yer, why nod go an see the funeral outside. He is a greadt man. Very tragic die. No, serious, go outside. He is yer. Day say he god over four unred cass lon. Jus imagine, four unred cass lon. Hool length of valley. Bess fighter you had. You god no respegt. When I was your age I saw Mussolini. Ubside down in Milan wid blood coming out of is head.

Luigi makes the silver machine puff and whistle. Bull tries on Nut's glasses. A fourth man comes through the door, tall, fair, odd clothes, badges over his denim jacket. He carries two black sacks. He stands holding an imaginary guitar,head raised, neck craning, eyes closed – a grim, ecstatic expression.

Luigi Allo, Rockee boy.

Nut Rock, Rock, the boy!

Bull Rockay! Hee hee, it's the Rockay!

Rock *Gyrating one leg, makes mouth music like a Hendrix guitar* Gee gee cacka gee gee cacka da da dee dee gee gee cacka dee dee dee ..smash! Hear them screaming? Rockay, Rockay! yeah! Yeah! *He produces a wreath from his sack and crowns himself.* Thanks! Thanks! O.K. you fans. O..K!
He pushes a clenched fist into the air. The group stare at the wreath.

Bull *Stands* Pass the flowers, Rock.

Rock Hold your head down.
Rock throws the wreath over Bull's head. Flowers break off. The three men throw flowers at each other. Rock goes into the sacks and breaks off more flowers.

Bull *Pushing flowers into Rock's mouth.* Flower Mouth.

Nut *Biting flower tops like a grenade pin.* Look out! Tomb! Toomb! *Rock and Bull snow flower each other. Nut puts a black sack over his head.* Hey,what's this boys? Whooo! Whooo! African ghost, mun. Whoo!
Rock and Bull take the opportunity of holding Nut in the bag.

Rock Bag of nuts. Bag of nuts for sale.

Nut *Muffled* Lay off, you thick lipped mullets. I can't breathe. I can't see. Boys, mun. I've got flowers in my eyes.

Bull Put him upside down like Muskotinee.

Rock Flower power up! *They raise him up.*

Luigi *Intervenes with a sweeping brush.* Boys! Stop! I'll fetch the police yer. Loog at der blutty mess by yer now. *Attempts to pick up flowers. Rock smacks them out of his hands.* You go outa my place. Go on.
Laughing, the three men move to another table. Luigi brushes up, takes the flowers to the back of the shop.

Nut Where you get them?

Rock I was coming up town. It's packed. So this bird comes out of the flower shop and she says, because I heard of the champ's death like, to carry these to the house. Right, I said. Now, they worth a few bob in it, the wreaths. So I thought, sell 'em to a wedding, right? Head screwed on, right? So I thought like, the boys will be in Weejees waiting for the Star to open. No! We could get more, you know. If we goes up the cemetery.

Nut You're getting more like a blond Dracula every day. Look at your teeth. You bloodsucking bag. It's wrong.

Bull The flowers will be soaking wet off the mountain. Your front room will be soaking wet with flowers. We'll have to keep 'em before we sell 'em, right?

Nut No, it's wrong. You bloodsuckers.

Rock Put the stinking flowers in Bull's house. No. No. His house is too dirty.Yeah. Yeah. Dutty scruffy 'ole.

Bull Shut up, Rock. My house is bigger than your house. And we got a garden. I'll smack your mouth, Rock.

Rock You got the dutty house with a tap outside. Heeee. Jungle bungalow. You haven't got a carpet. Only oilcloth. And they gob on the floor.

Bull Look at your wife then. She's a boot. She's only like that. *Holds up one straight finger.*

Rock Know what the kids call your house? Know? Uh? Know? Manure house. Know that?

Bull You're the girl, Rock. Girlie. Why don't you wear nice lipstick *purses his lips* and get your hair done *smooths his hair.* Your wife's like that. *Holds his finger up again..*

Rock They kick you out of jail because you were cheating.

Bull I wore a uniform. You had nothing.

Rock You had a dirty gypsy mother, eight kids, a lodger, your father was a cider waller, and you all lived in two rooms. Children pwpping in the corner on paper on dutty flagstones.

Bull Look at your wife then, like a peg, she's like a stick of rock and she had her teeth out. Hold on, hold it! My wife could smack your wife and put her in hospital in two minutes.

Rock Your wife's so fat she stinks and squeaks with wet pee

legs. You can hear her coming. *Bull nastily stares.* You're not King for long, lovely boy. I'll put you down.
Rock points his finger close to Bull's mouth. Bull bites the finger. Both men stand aggressively.

Nut *Leaping up, holds them apart and talks to an imaginary audience.* I've had a gutsful,right? Of you two. He thinks he's King of the streets *nods to Bull*, the best fighter in town, and he *nods to Rock* he thinks he's bloody Prince next in line! You couple of fat farts, you. You big girls' blouse. Luigi!

Luigi *Back of the shop* War you want, Nud?

Nut Time, Luigi!

Luigi Bout five to one.

Nut Star's open at two. Let's just wait, you Delroys.
Nut and Bull sit.

Rock I'll be King one day-ay, hmmmm hmmm dip dap dee crack smack a lack lee. Hmm.

Bull to *Rock* Hey! Hey! Oi! See this? This? Oi! This look! *Points to his mouth.* See this. Uh? Ai! This, right. Button it! Button it like! OK? Right? Hey! This right? Mouth! Keep it shut! Oi! Shut it! Oi! Shut it! This!
Prods his mouth, prods Rock's mouth. An excited Luigi appears from the back room.

Luigi Boys, boys! I dink dar funeral's yer!

Nut Boys! The funeral!
Bull, Rock and Nut rush out..

Luigi *Following* Dew, dew. Iss alike the war in a way.
Outside more figures against the glass. The cafe is empty. Shadows and figures continue to pass the window.

Luigi *Enters, shouts back at the door* First car will be yer now in a minute! *Takes off his apron.* Hey! *to the door.* Who a turner my sign? I lose business!

Nut *Appears at the door* The Rocky boy did. But shut your gob, Luigi *he fingers Luigi's jaw* or Bull and Rock won't give the little ole proteckto, proteckto, you know? Little ole protection. Know what I mean, Uh? Protection? Is the Nut right, right? Have the boys been good?

Luigi Yeah, der boys bin good. Dey stop Bill Stigs an hiss boys from breaking der door.

Nut There you are, you immigrant. They protect the community. Is the Nut right? Right?
Rock and Bull appear at the door. A scuffling. Luigi stands on his chair.

Rock Liar. Liar. You never seen a black, let alone speak to one. Only on the box you seen 'em.

Luigi Boys! Boys! Fewneral be yer now!

Bull Ugly. They're all ugly. I hates 'em.

Luigi Iss one o'clock boys. Boys? Iss five pass one. Fewneral coming *jumps off his chair and hurries out, stopping by the gang. Eyes them with that suspicious look.* Ai! Iss gone one o'clock boys. Nut! Fewneral!
Exits. The dark conflab is unresponsive. Nut is preaching and wagging a finger, a bee in and out of the dark flower.

Nut Boys. Hour's time, we'll all have a drink. Take it easy. Come on.

Bull *Standing* I saw him once, right? *Points to the window* That hero in a bastard box. He was like this, look. *Bull jogs around the cafe and shadow boxes on his tour.* He knows me, right? See? Knows all about me. *Points to Rock.* He says, how be, Bull? Right? So he stops. Stops and comes over. *Walks back to the group.*

Rock *Quickly.* Liar! Big liar! Girl! Nancy! *stands. Sways his hips and walks effeminately.*

Nut Rap up! Rap up! *Head in hands in anguish pose.* Sit down , Bull. Sit down, Rockee love.
Bull laughs, points at Rock. They sit.

Bull *Looking at the two heads turned away* He didn't look well to me. *No response.* Looked like he was going to be sick.

Silence.

Rock He was always sick. It was inside man, from birth. One day that stinking weakness.....stinking weakness was going to catch him *holds his throat* by the throat. *Rock strangles himself. Shouting* The bigger they are! The harder they fall! *He falls.*

Nut *Angry*. Get up, thin neck! Listen. *Nut turns to the window. Crowds are appearing. Turns back.* It was a flaw. *Rock and Bull bend in.* Like in a fault.... I had on a gun. Airgun. On the barrel. *Nut holds a rifle.* Down the barrel. *They look.* About there! About a third down. *Nut indicates the flaw.* One day for no reason, it snapped! A beautiful gun. *Nut snaps the barrel.* The flaw got it. A cold night and snap! *Snaps it again.* That's what he had.
The three look at the window silently.

Bull Go on. Keep going.

Nut Snap! In two.
Nut looks at the gun. Bull and Rock look at his hands. Nut hands one piece to Bull, another to Rock. Both receive it.. Nut collapses on to the floor in silent laughter, pointing to Rock and Bull holding the gun sections. Outside, figures crowd at the window. The sound of a male voice choir. A sad, slow hymn..

Bull *Smacking Nut.* Liar!

Rock *Kicking Nut.* Liar! *Nut groans and rolls on his back. Dead In The Movies. Choir sings.*

Bull *Kneeling, opens Nut's eye.* I didn't hit him hard *To his ear* Nut! Nut! Nut! Nut!
Shakes him. No response from Nut.

Luigi *Rushing in* Boys! Boys! Come an see der singing. *Looks at the floor* Get Nut offa my floor. Asprin behind der counter.
Luigi rushes back outside. The choir sound near.

Rock *Bending, touches Nut gently and cat smooths his tan.* You kicked him, Bull!

Bull You kicked him, Rock!

Rock You hit him, then!

Bull You kicked him then!

Rock You caused it!

Bull And you!

Rock I was only playing.

Bull *Quietly* And me.

Rock Jesus Christ. I didn't think I was that strong.

Bull It must have been me, Rock. I hit him first.

Rock I must have finished him off.

Nut moves slightly and opens his mouth. Rock and Bull bend closer. Choir are nearer.

Nut *Softly, choked.* Tell...

Luigi *Appears, excited* Boys! Quick! You see nuttin. *Looks at Nut* Carry him oud.
Luigi rushes off. Rock and Bull are close to Nut's face.

Nut *Death groan shout.* Tell!... Tell!

Rock & Bull Uh? What? What, tell?

Nut *Quietly* Tell lor.

Rock Teller? Tailor?

Bull *Props Nut's head with his arm* Teller What?

Nut Tell.... Teller, Tell lor.

Rock Tellor? Micky Tailor?

Bull Crazy. Two deaths! Him out there *looks at window* him in here *looks at Nut. To Rock with malice.* You hit him Rock!

Nut *Choked* Tell-or-ai...

Rock Tell Laura? High? Dope? Where? What Laura?

Nut *Holds their faces, sings through clenched teeth.* Tell Laura I love her, Tell Laura I need her, Da da dee dee dum dum, something something, I just can't wait....
Nut rolls away laughing. The choir are outside.

Bull Nut! Nut, my little Nut! Hey, hey, hey!
Nut revolves on the floor laughing and finally kicks Rock's leg.

Rock What's that for?

Nut To remind you. *Kicks again.*

Rock I'll take you to the moon with a hook. *Shows his fist.*

Nut Bull!

Bull *Steps forward to defend.* Take me Rock instead.

Rock *Nastily* Don't hide behind Bull, slob! *Pauses* One night when it's all quiet, you can hear the pavements clicking, and it's raining, and there's no-one in the world left, I'll be there, Nut. Waiting for you.
Rock walks away in temper and strums chords. Choir fades. Nut, turning, kicks Bull.

Bull Hey, little man!

Nut Just testing.

Bull *Lifting Nut from the ground* Test again little boy!

Nut *Kicks and quickly* Testing, Bull. Whether you can take it. Take a smack? Right? Nut right? *Pauses.* You're so strong, bum guts, bum tits. *Bull laughs, flattered. Choir in distance. A stream of silhouettes on the window.* Come here, Rock. *Rock moves sullenly. Nut raises their arms as champions.* Now then, who's the guy who gets the money? Uh? Who's the guy who says, Bull's coming for you, Rocky's coming for you! Uh? Me. Right? I'm the guy. OK? I'm the front man. Who's the guy who says to the punters, oh! Oh! They're after me as well! What do I say?

Bull *Quietly* After you as well.

Nut Right! You spittoon. So I says to them, hey, I says, I owes Bull and Rock thirty bucks as well! They're after me! So they says, hey Nut, we'll give you thirty sweet peas, we clears your debt, you put in a good word for us, OK? So I come back with thirty cool ones. I shares with you equal, don't I?

Rock Yeah yeah, you're straight, man.

Nut So I goes back to the punters, says it's OK! Boys are not coming to get you. Everything ace! AOK! I'm happy, they're happy, you're happy. So I get fed up with protection sometimes, I gotta lash out. *Drops their arms.* What? Two kicks? You'll get more than two kicks in a minute!

Nut kicks their backsides. They run, they laugh, to the back of the cafe and hold a table and chairs in mock defence.

Luigi At *the door, kneeling, beseeching.* Woss a madder? *Gesticulates.* Choir sings. Lovely peace. Gread man goes away.

You crazy... no respect... you liddle people.... *Pauses.* You end up in jail! *Exit quickly.*

Nut *Shouting.* Come and see me they should, spaghetti! Little nothing men should take the applause! *Nut holds out his arms horizontally. Rock and Bull carry him. His arms fold into ballet pose.* Company.. to the window-oooooh!

Bull What can you see Nut?

Nut *Heavenly, hands in prayer.* The two most beautiful angels in white, with wings apiece, and a big, black boxer seven feet tall. Go get them, Fang! *They drop Nut and rush through the door. Nut bolts the door, runs through Luigi's room and bolts the back entrance. He returns, searching through his pockets.* Come on speedy coke. Speed me. Brands Hatch me, my little shooting stars. *Faces at door, shouting, banging.* Shut up, three heads! You busy Barclays! You Tory wets! *Finds a packet.* Ah! my speedo-cokey. *Unfolds, sniffs a line on the counter and swallows the rest greedily. Figures bang, then disappear. Nut leans against the counter and slides down slowly into a sitting position- a broken doll. Banging at the back door.* Shut up, you animals! Get off my back. Don't crowd me. *Holds his neck.* I'm going backwards man! *Pauses.* What's this? I'm going backwards. What kind of cokey-speedo is this? *Holds his head tighter.* This is opposite speed! This is action replay! Jeezus. *Pulls his head forward and crumples into a heap.* This is reverse coma. *Pauses, shakes his head. Faces, tapping at the door.* Go away tramps! Beggars! Victoria scum! *Kneeling, shivering.* I'm scared. *To the window.* Stop staring! I'm doing my thing! I'm alone, I'm dying, man. I'm a little island. No man is an island. No man is a Barry Island. *Banging. Shouts.* No man is a Barry Island! *Laughs to himself and it turns to sobs.* What would I get, uh? I could die like the hero, on the floor, with nothing. *Pauses. Faces disappear.* One flower. One car. *Moans. Takes off his glasses, sobs quietly.* I got no chance. Strangle town. I gotta get out. Dumpton! *The sound of the back door breaking. Nut rises, replacing his glasses.* Here he comes, the Bull. *In imitation.* You OK Nut? Nut! My Nut! Nut! All so swinging obvious. *Bull appears. Nut silences him with a finger to the mouth.* Nut? My little Nut, you OK Nut?

Bull *Walks forwards, with compassion.* No, no, I'm Bull. You are Nut.
Rock and Luigi appear. Rock springboards on the emotion.

Rock *Wild guitar singing.* Let me come and set you free, on the streets of Luigi's cafe, yeah!

Luigi *Slow and deliberate.* My door. We break my door in. Nut! Whassa madder? Where ew sense? *Pauses* Iss my property. I worg hard. You godt no respectd, nod tha much. *shows a small amount with his fingers.* You pay boy, you pay me dis time!

Rock What time's the Star open, Luigi?

Bull What time is it open?

Luigi Shud up! Thas jus a trick.

Nut *Pulling money from his pocket.* Five bucks. Blood money. I'll give you five bucks.
Gives Luigi a five pound note. Rock and Bull sit down. Rock practices, Bull puts his head on the table.

Luigi I give you change. Doo pounds. No no, doo pounds for a new latch, tree pounds for labour *waves the note* I need all dis, Nud!

Nut *Waves him away.* Rock! Pumping Rust. Bull! Lord of the Boot. You got to listen to me. *He sits with the boys. Luigi chinks the till.* We got to change, boys.

Luigi Change? You better go, go away! Go away! Jus go way. Worg- lige I god to worg.

Nut OK OK OK OK, Luigi.

Luigi Nod jus O'gay O'gay O'gay. Whad you pud inna live you ged oud of id. Simble! You pudding in nuttin, jus taking. *Pauses.* An' at grazzy fightdin. Dun ged yous anywhere. *Walks over to the set piece.* You 'member. You! *Prods Nut.* Like a small kidt, come yer taking pasals for yew farder. Jus a kidt, ten, twelve. You nice boy, polite, bid cheegy, O'gay. I give rassberry an' ice a lod.

Nut Yeah yeah yeah!

Luigi You say yeah yeah yeah! You say O'gay O'gay O'gay an' you turn round an log me oudt! My bag door smassed in! You throw flowers, you dun clean ub! *Pauses* An' you say yeah yeah yeah, thas all you say. Why you bodder wid dees two? *The gang* *look elsewhere, laughing.* You godt gift of der gab, you could godt somewheres, mun. *Pauses* Whad we talg about you for, uh? On a day lige dis! *Points to the window.* He struggle hard. Issa tragedy. He give his bess. You 'magine being on der floor, uh? Flad oudt. *Pauses.* I noss sayin he shouldna gone to 'Merica. Maybe he had a weakness.

Nut *In irritation.* A flaw, man, a flaw!

Luigi So whad! Mace no difference whad it was, he done iss bess!

Nut *Still irritated.* Don't give me rabbit, Luigi, or I'll let Billy Sticks bust this, this useless cafe in half, OK Cornetto?

Luigi *Throws his towel over his shoulder.* You talg Billy Stigs. You big talg protection. Issa game. I feel sorry for you. You godt nuttin. *Shouts.* Who you tink you are, uh? Al Cabone? Uh? Uh? Uh? *Rock and Bull shake with laughter. Luigi walks to them.* Loog ad dem now! Fightdin all der time, big boys now! Billy der Kidt! Flamin cowboys! I godt photos. One say, Howard Jones, Btis A.B.A. *Points at Bull.*

Nut *Laughs* How can you name a baby Howard Jones? Little baby, all in white, that long *shows length* Name? Howard Jones! *Bull collapses with laughter.*

Luigi Loog at this one. *Points at Bull.* Photos lige dis. *Poses in a boxing guard.* Says Clifton Richards, *Looks up and indicates a name in lights* prospect for der future.

Nut Yeah sure! What did they get? Nothing. Look at the hero boy outside. What did he get? Sick FA! *Luigi walks back behind the counter. Nut walks over, meets him across the counter.* Do something uh? I was a nice kid uh? What did they call me? Hmm? Snake eyes. Yeah, snake eyes! And that moved to reptile. Yeah, that's what they called me, reptile! Reptile! I'm stuck with it for life.

Luigi *Somewhat sympathetic* Iss only kids' names.

Nut Yeah, I'm marked for life! Keep calling a kid reptile and he becomes a reptile.

Luigi No, iss only a name. Jus kids.

Nut No way!

Luigi *Stands on a chair and looks out of the window.* I wadch der memory of a real man!

Nut Yeah! Jingle bells, Batman smells.

Luigi I dun know whad ew mean mun!

Nut Here's the tragedy, Luigi. In here! Give us the flowers now, Luigi. Give us the flowers now! This is the new war, jobless, hopeless, pissy! Dead soldiers stuck together, slit smiles like dead sheep. *Slits his face.* Give us the flowers now! When we can still smell 'em.

Luigi *Walks to the crowd of three as he puts on his apron.* Loog you. When high came, over on der boad, doo weegs yer, day pud me in jail. Yeah, jail. Nineteen fordy. Yeah. Smashing my place, smashing my farder, jus because high was Italian. *Circles them.* High bin through id Nud. High nod sorry for myself. *Firm and tight fisted.* You godda fight bag, high know Nud. Jus lee me alone. High feel sorry for you all, mun. Das why I led you come yer, mun. *Pauses and straightens himself.* Time iss had. Very had. No good bein alcoholic and druggy boys.

Nut We've joined Alcoholics Conspicuous Luigi.

Luigi Das why you godt terrorists an' blagshirds an' Nasses. Loog, Nud. An' you boys. High bin through id. High loog aver you all mun. Through thig an' thin, mun.*Pauses* Laydly high bin dreamin about der war every night. I godt no family, Nud, jus me. *Dismisses the crowd with a wave of his hand.* Iss all crazy feelins today. Iss mad! You wanna argew, high argew bag. High nod stupid, mun! Go an' join der Labour Party. *Ducks down behind counter.*

Nut Yeah, sure, up the fucking maternity hospital! *A long silence. Looking up.* Stupid lights Luigi. Or am I depressed? *Luigi brings out binoculars and cleans them. Looks through and adjusts. His dark binocular eyes survey the room. Bull is clicking and snapping his teeth continuously, violently.* What's that, then?

Bull Skull Laffing. *Snap, snap, snap.*

Nut Skull laughing? Good joke, Bull. Your first ever. Coming on, boys. *Turns sharply to Luigi.* I got the words, he got the songs, he's got the muscle. All human life here, lovely boy! This is it! *Nut sits disgruntled, sneers at the two boys opposite. They stare back stupidly, expectantly, Bull with a faint trace of teeth snapping.*What am I going to do with you? *No response.* Jesus what am I going to do? *Thinks.* We got to call it off, I'm sick of our team. Crazy!

Luigi *Standing at the window with binoculars.* Yeah, you crassie oright.

Nut What's the time, Luigi?

Luigi Star's open in fordy minutes. Hey! Der's big Miggy Flynn, der wrestler. Das his wife. Mus be. An' der mayor.

Nut *Shakes his head.*You must have been a baby once, Bull. You rimp.

Rock He was left deserted man, on a doorstep. In a skip.

Nut *Smiling.* I bet you beat up other babies. *Bull laughs.* You were never a baby, Rockee slut. You were sicked up from outer space.

Rock *Stands, legs gyrate a la Elvis.* Sicked up, da da da da, outer space, da da da da, he's the boy who takes the world, dumm dumm dumm.

Nut Shut up, Rock, shut up! Sit down! You stupid mental bogs. *Leans forward.* Don't do the routine on me sweetneck. Keep it for the suckers. I'm on an opposite trip today, Rockington. *A long pause of total boredom.* Your boy Wayne go to school, Bull?

Bull Yeah. All the time.

Nut Liar !

Bull Why?

Nut Liar! He hasn't been there, liar. Since September, liar.

Bull He's been there, boy!

Nut Liar! *Pulls out a piece of paper.* What's this then? *Waves the paper, opens it, and stretches over at Bull. Bull snatches, misses.* Liar! He hasn't been there, liar-liar. I saw him this morning, crying in the crowd outside. They didn't believe him in school. Been given the stick for lying. Liar! Like his daddy. Picking coal on the mountain, he's been. Picking iron and buckets and decaying cookers, stinking prams, dead sheep and persil boxes. Liar! He never goes.

Bull Dun you read that in front of him!

Nut *Smiles sneakily and reads.* Dear Mr Withers. Wayne haven't been in school till now for his father got a bad head when he dived through the headboard of the bed for he thought Wayne

was drowning in his sleep. He will be home helping me to do the house his father in hospital with a skull illness still. Mrs Jones.
Rock collapses in laughter.

Bull It's the truth mun, Nut!

Nut *Folding the paper.* Liar!

Bull You're going too far, little man!

Nut *Leans to Bull.* I got the mouth. You're sunk without the mouthpiece.

Rock *Holding his crutch, laughing.* I gotta go man. I gotta go for a gypsy's kiss! *Stumbles off.*

Luigi *Turns and looks at Rock through binoculars.* Pull der chain aver you!

Nut You go to school, Bull?

Bull Yeah, twice. *Laughs at his own joke.*

Nut Look at me now, look at my lips. Watch Nut's lips. See Nut's lips moving? *Bull collapses laughing. Nut adjusts his chair like a teacher.* Howard? Howard? Listen Howard.

Bull *Laughing but nervous.* No don't, don't mun! Don't do the teacher, Nut!

Nut *Menacing, leans to Bull.* Howard, look at me. I mean it! *Bull looks, keeping a straight face.* Now, Howard. *Nut raises a finger. Bull collapses. Nut turns his chair and sits cowboy style.* Bull! *Bull looks up. With sardonic kindliness.* Today, Howard, we are going to study opposites. Opposites, right? *Bull nods, dull.* Opposites, Howard. *Pauses.* What is opposite to ... wait for it..up? *Bull, suddenly nervous, shakes his head and slowly bows it down.* Jesus. Bull boy really thinks it's school.

Luigi *Staring outside.* Lee him alone, Nud.

Nut Shut up dunce! Corner dunce! This is my school. *Pauses.* Down. Is the opposite, Howard. Down. *Stands and enjoys his new power, stalks Bull.* What is opposite to in, Howard?

Bull *Quietly* Inside

Nut Pardon, Howard? Pardon? Speak up!

Bull *Coughs* Inside.

Nut *Still patronising in a macabre fashion.* No, Howard. Out is the opposite of in.

Luigi *Turning* Outd. Yes I godt tha one!

Nut *Turns his chair back and sits near Bull.* Now then, Howard. *Bull is very nervous.* Men in white are coming for you. Gypsy will take you away. Blackman will run off with your mother. Bogey ghost is coming. *Louder.* God is watching! Teacher's watching!

Bull Stop it mun, stop it!

Luigi *Without turning.* Craszy as a cake wid nuds in it.

Nut What is the opposite of.... pigeon?

Luigi You god gift of der gab you have.

Nut Opposite of pigeon, Howie? *Stands and walks around Bull.* I'm brill, Luigi, just brill! Pigeon, Howard. *Taps Bull's head.* Opposite of pigeon, Howie? Opposite of pigeon, dum dum! Dum dum! *Shouts.* What's the opposite of pigeon?

Bull Fish. I dun know!

Nut No, Howard, *tapping again* you dense plank, you daft bat! Mud! Mud! Is the opposite of pigeon! *Changes his tone. Softly.* What's the opposite of pigeon, Howie?

Bull *Standing.* Mud!

Nut *Quickly.* Go to the back of the class, immediately, you fifteenth rate beast!

Bull *Sadly follows Nut's finger, settles into a corner. Pointing at Nut.* Could a dog fight a badger?

Nut Shut up! I'm the teacher, I ask the questions. This is my class!

Luigi Claz? What claz? Dis iss a cavay. My cavay! *Rock appears.* Oh no. The mennal patient now. Oh no!

Nut Sit down, Rock. *Rock sits.* Stands up, Rock! *Rock stands in "cool" pose.* Remember you went to hospital? Broke down face, thirty-eight stitches?

Rock Yeah man! Stuffed doll, stuffer racker, stuffer racker om pom slice! *Slits his face with a finger, gyrates his leg.*

Nut This is a talent contest, right? OK, Presley neck, do the imitations of what you saw! *Folds his arms and leans back.*

Luigi *Staring outside.* Lodda women crying an kids

Rock *Full flight.* Hospital! *Glamourous indication of size.* Me! *Terrorist pose.* Cuts! *Sickly act.* Doctor! *Aloof, show off.* People! *Mimes injuries.* Operation! *Sees the heavens, on bended knee.* Staff nurse! *Hitleresque.* Needle! *Silent film horror.* Stitches! *Woman knitting.* Wheelchair! Aah! *Loving mother.* Bed! *Sexual action.* Undressing! *Arm movement of snake ending at crutch* Holds nurse! *Bumper fun.* Cripples! *Hobbles.* Me! *Bended knee, worships the star.* A star is dead! A star is dead! Ohhh!

Nut *Squealing with delight.* Tops! Tops! You go on a tops course! You win Rock, top talent. *To imaginary audience through microphone.* And he's still alive folks, and living in the valleys!

Luigi Tob, uh? Tob mennal patient. *To the window.* Loog. Benny Mazders. Televisun man. He loog der same. He came.

Nut Dead soldiers here, Luigi! Right, my turn now. *Stands.*

Luigi You dun know nuttin about soltiers, an' about jops lige you said. You dun effer worg. You godt gifd of der gab, a big moufth, jus der gifd of der gab.

Nut Shut up pope of hope!

Luigi Yeah! Now I see why famous peeble can ged shod, peeble lige you. Thas where der blagshirds come from, Nassees! *In imitation.* Me now, me now! Uh! Terrorisds. Jus easy talgk, jus bored oudt of der skull!

Nut I told you, Luigi. *Finger to his lips* Proteckto.

Luigi *Nasty, stepping down.* Yez, you toldt me. High fight you bag one day. High nod so small. High god Mario

Nut He'll have to bring the Mafia, kid!

Luigi Mario, he geds war he wands!

Nut Maybe baby. My turn now! Me now! You got your own business, Luigi bee gee, I got mine. Now. In this shit hole. I make good of a bad number, OK?

Luigi Lige high said, too many films!

Nut Yeah, and you're watching that box too much!

Rock What you going to do, Nut?

Nut Woodstock, right?

Bull Right!

Nut Yeah! Woodstock's dead, Vietnam lives. Bullets beat the peace! My show is about power. Not your power, Bull, big hard town. Not yours, Rock, *points to his head* living up there you are, fifteen years ago! Not Luigi's war power, Ok wireless? 'Itler! Not Itma Luigi, 'Itler!.

Luigi You gone crazy. Der's der real power oudsidte, peeble togeder!

Nut *Shakes head, hits it on the table.* Crazy? Uh? *Imitation.* Higha craszy uh?

Luigi O yez, you gone crazy o'right.

Nut Me crazy? What you looking at hmm? Effing funeral. Be end and end all. We're alive man, alive and kicking. Give us the flowers now, Luigi. Bastarding Italians! Same as the Welshies, no wonder you don't push off. Crazy Catholics! You didn't give that boy, *points to the window* that boy, you didn't give that boy time of day! Not when he was trying, not when he was alive and trying! No flowers then.

Luigi Whad you mean, Nud?

Nut You used to say, look at that skinny kid. He got no chance. Nice boy, wears a bobble hat, nice boy, nice boy. He don't stand a chance, he's only a valleys' boy. You give him nothing Luigi. Look at you now. Great hero this, fat hero that,yeah. When he's dead! Typical of this town. Looking for heroes when they die! You got no guts to believe them. Not when they were trying, when they had the energy, man!

Luigi Get outa my place. Get out!

Nut Yeah, yeah! Join the club, Luigi gee gee, join the nothing club, nothing! *Holds his hands to his head screaming.* Join the death spell club. This whole dump is death spell club! You got no faith in shit man, no faith! *Emotional* Look at us. Look at him Rock, in Mars over there. Look at him Bull. I was called snake eyes. What chance have I got eh? Give me nothing and I'll be nothing. This whole town, right? This whole valley, right? Shapes you up, gives you piss! This whole cowing country. Stink Wales! Death spell man, death spell! You killed us all, Luigi! Looking for heroes! *Exhausted, he turns.*

Luigi *Quietly.* When der Star open, big drinkin club, you stay there, Nud. Dun you ever come bag. Dun you ever come bag again!

Bull *Rising, emotional.* I coulda been great Luigi. I coulda been world champ!

Nut You could have been great, Bull, really great. There was no faith around, boy. How d'you expect to have it yourself? Hmmm? Do you understand, Bull? *Watches Bull shadow boxing.* Bull? *Bull stops.* Do us a real favour. Put your head on the desk. Go to sleep. I'll wake you in twenty minutes. Do that for me?
Bull does it.

Rock *Mimes a slow, sad guitar break.* Nut? Whole world's a rock show man. Everything's rock, right? Like this is rock now. *Strums.* Gimme words to use. Go on, any words man. Everything's a rock song. Know what I mean?

Nut *Head down.* Yes, Rock..

Rock Everything's, like, rock.

Nut Yes, love.

Rock We're living in a cool show.

Nut Yes, Rockee love.

Rock Gimme a statement. Like, anything.

Nut Fuck off, Rock.

Rock *After a brief pause, strums and poses.* Fuckeroff Rockee butt! Ucker fucker ocky cocky rocky beat! Jicker rockoff, fucker rocky dock.

Nut You're going to get the psychiatric gold award, that's what you're getting.

Rock Middle eight, total contrast, listen. *Strums and sings.* Rocky lived in a magic zoo, an all the beasts around him, carnival of death, o yeah, carnival of death. *Singing.* Get out Rock. Leave the zoo. Make your way in the world. *Singing.* Fuckeroff Rockee butt! Ucker, fucker, ocky, cocky, rocky, beat! Yeah! Get it Nut? Cool man.

Nut *Sitting and despondent.* Go and check Bull. He could be dead. Search his hair for nits. I bet he's got biceps on his scalp. *Rock checks Bull. Bull wakes.* What's the time, Luigi?

Luigi *Without turning.* Time you went.

Bull Put it there, Rock. *Holds his arm for Indian wrestling.*

Rock *Jumps back.* Godzilla versus Dracula, Dracula versus me, me versus the world, and I pick it up and go. Dam, susp, boof, gustegen, the world shatters! You want to take me on now? I pick up the world man! I'm god!

Bull You're a big kid.

Rock Heard about that kid born with four legs? Mother was a goat.

Bull I don't know him. Put it there Rock. *Holds his arm. Rock clasps. Bull wins.* I beat god! God is just a little kid.

Rock *Angry.* You're so ugly, Bull, I got to walk away.

Nut *Standing silent. Grows out of his mood, slaps his face.* OK boys, come here.
They choose a table and sit. Nut hands out tablets secretly. Shadows on the window and movement of people outside. A knock at the door. Luigi stands on his toes, hunches his shoulders, raises his arm.

Luigi *Loud whisper.* Shud dill doo o'glog! I shud dill doo o'glog! Go way! High shamed to led anybody in. Iss lige a morgue in yer. *He stares and recognises the faces at the door.* Holt on! *Opens the door.* Come In. *Enter two men. The first is fortyish, white hair, black coat, black tie, grey pinstriped suit, black shoes. The second is black, early twenties. A welterweight in a light suit and black tie, black arm band. Quietly.* Dun mind me asking. You are Jacky Sims an' that Billy Flowers? How do you do. I seen all oz you fightds, Billy. *Billy smiles.* You want some tea?.

Jacky Coffee twice. *A cockney.*
Billy goes to a table, looks around, quiet confidence and expects recognition. Jacky pays.

Luigi You wan to eat?

Jacky No, you know, special diet for the boy.

Luigi Oh yez, yez. *Takes the money.* You come for der hero's farewell uh? Sad business, what yew say?

Jacky *Moving with coffee.* Sad blow to the fight game. Real sad blow. *Coffee on table.* This is the only place that would let us in. The whole town has closed up. We missed our car in the procession. But we come to pay respect. That's the least we could do.

Luigi Iss respectd for the boy.

Jacky Yeah, a fine tribute man. Seems like you take a special interest in your fighters.

Luigi Hool town mun, all is fightding. Bin fightding for unred years. Aye, first fightders widdout gloves, on der mountains. Fightdin all der time. Price- fightders. Famous town. Old iron town. Big boggers. I come from Italy, to come away from bogsin family and fightding in der streeds wi guns, Mussolini you know? Bagshirds. An' I come yer an' dey still fightdin. For nuttin. Nasurally fightdin. Thas why dey bogsin now.

Jacky Yeah, there's a lot to know about small towns like this. Surprising what you learn.

Luigi Small town, uh? Whas a London, uh? You got a migsture of blood, in it? Issa cosmopolitan, yeah? We same. Small town, uh!

Jackie OK, man. Nice coffee.

Billy Like the man says, nice coffee. *Holds Jackie in a quiet conversation.*

Nut What time the pubs open, Luigi?

Luigi Doo o'glog. Yew know dat, Nud.

Nut What's the time now, Luigi?

Luigi Twenny five do doo.

Nut *Beckons to Luigi.* Your telephone. In the kitchen. I don't know, I thought I heard it. I don't know, mind. Can you hear it from here?

Luigi *Listening.* Issa telephone. Issa Mario. You know what. Please Luigi, high'm short, no money, high skintd. Bet ew now.
Luigi leaves. Nut walks to the two strangers and picks up their coffees.

Billy We haven't finished.

Nut No, no, I'm not collecting. I'm going to serve you. Look, you are visitors, OK? And you mean to tell me you had to carry the coffees yourself? This is how it should be done. Right? Like this. *Walks over dignified and lays down the cups.* Your coffees, sir.

Jacky Thanks. You needn't have bothered.

Nut It's OK, it's OK. It's OK. *Smiles like a landlady. The two men stare back confidently. Nut smiles, nods his head. The men nod back, continue in conversation. Nut snaps his fingers. Billy* *stares confidently. Nut points at Billy and smiles, withdraws his hand, puts it under his arm and makes a grunt. Jackie, with a slight wave of his hand, holds Billy back. Luigi returns to a silence and stares.* Two coffees, Luigi.

Luigi OK, Nut.

Rock *Singing.* Bananas, bananas. Give the monkey bananas. *Bull stares stupidly.* If the man took a lunge at you in the dark he'd bite half your face away.

Nut *Picks up the coffees and places them on the visitors' table.* Jacky Sims. Right? Billy Flowers. Right? Right boys,we can't offer you a drink. But as a mark of respect, two coffees, right? Us boys to you. Fighters to fighters. We're real glad you came. Thanks, boys. *Jacky nods his head with a confused stare. Someone knocks the door.* Time, Luigi?

Luigi Twenny do doo!
Nut mouths 'Fuck off' at the window. In the background the dark flower opens. Bull and Rock move next to Nut.

Bull Don't you know me?

Jacky No.

Nut Don't you know this Man?

Bull I'll make him mental. I'll smack him Nut.

Nut *Puts his arm around Bull.* This is Bull. A real character. A real good boy. Show them, Bull. *Bull dances a little, spars, a quick punch in the air.* Bull is a natural. Know what I mean? Been to Swansea and Cardiff University.

Rock He couldn't pass a fucking biscuit. Couldn't pass my fucking house.

Nut Shut up, Rock. To study robbery with violence. Nine 'O' levels in police punches. Five "A' levels in smash and grabbing. Lectured on buttmanship throughout Wales. Introduced to doctors, philosophers and trick cyclists.

Luigi Cobbers wride about him in deir boogs.

Nut He's the contender for the universal street championship.

Rock And me, I'm the Prince.

Nut Excuse him. He's got more hang-ups than the history of capital punishment. He runs his own show in there. *Points to his head. Puts his arm around Rock.* This character is Rock.

Bull Rockay ay!

Nut He's the Prince. He takes the boys through the trips. Trip? Acid? Zoom! Rock is in outer space, boy, he's in the dark universe. Tell them Rock.

Rock I've seen fire and I've seen rain. And I've seen peacocks in tunnels in Boots. I've seen the true God, man, he's shining white, and I saw him on a throne of burning gold and brass and yellow streaks and silver flames, in twenty-two George Street. And I've seen statues that come alive and navy-blue tigers and ships in the air and boats in the dock, and loads of coppers climbing ladders through the clouds.

Jacky Very interesting. Some other time perhaps.

Nut Sit down, Cracky Pims.

Billy I'll sort them. I'll sort them.

Nut Think about your licence, Billy Roses.

Luigi Loss of characters, in it, Nut. You god Dai Redt, Dai Blackg, Dai Blackg and Blue, Dai Whitde, Dai Green.

Nut He lives in a field.

Bull *Laughs*. And Dai Crack, Master of Filth.

Rock I've never heard of Dai Green.

Nut Dai Green who lives on the mountain? No?

Rock No.

Nut Baby's life, Rock. My baby's life. Dai green.

Luigi Show der visidors some ruckby, boys.

Nut Yeah, we got rugby! Show 'em boys.
Rock and Bull pack down awkwardly. Nut throws in a cup as a ball, both men heel it.

Jacky Impressive, but we're off.

Billy My head's going man, my head's going.

Jacky Come on, Billy. What's the matter?

Nut *Quickly.* Boys! Sing some Welsh songs, boys.
Billy sways. Manager is at his wits' end.

Rock and Bull *To the tune of the national anthem.* Glad! I'm glad! Ply him with rover I'm glad. Roy veen, puff bye, I'm yer, yewer there. Plied yn cross galleon, I'm glad.
Luigi and Nut clap. Manager is pop eyed.

Rock *Takes the floor.* Kuthero bompei mae clitog. Kew suffig him grimp, simpla wisby sum gump, high gusby trogly yap yap.
Nut, Bull and Luigi clap.

Nut Good Welsh Rock, well done kid. Imitations now!

Bull I got one. Who's this? *Raises his trousers.* You dutty pig. You dutty cow.

Nut Rat. You dirty rat, you cusp! Cagney. Jimmy Cagney, right?

Luigi Gread! Who's diss? *Leans backwards and paws the air.* Uh? Who dat?

Bull Dead cat.

Rock Dead spider.

Nut Someone climbing a ladder.

Luigi No! Iss Chatton Heston in Acony and der Eggstasy. Iss Michelangelo painin der ceilin.

Nut Shut up, Luigi!

Luigi You god Max Boyce in Soud Wales, we god Michelangelo painin der ceilin in Italy.
Billy's head is lolling.

Jacky Get a glass of water for this boy.

Luigi You wan asprin, uh?

Rock *Singing.* I can feel it coming in the air today, oh Nut. And I've been waiting for this moment in the cafe-ay-ay, Luigi. Can you feel it coming...

Nut *During the performance.* Crisp and coolly, Rock, crisp and coolly, boy. Yeah, crisp-ey an' a cool-ley. *To the manager.* The boys are, you know, not feeling well. The funeral. They were good boys, you know? They used these a lot. *Shows a fist.*

Jacky *Attempts to stand up and haul Billy. Billy is heavy and swaying.* Look. I'll send tickets. Three of you. Straight up. Come up. Couple of fights, do the town, see the girls, a few clubs, on me. Take it easy boys. Billy got the Euro in two months, he needs a rest. Have a night on me. You know, perhaps you boys need time out from this old town, see the world. Come on, everybody's upset. It's a sad day.

Luigi Yeah, you boys go up to London. Iss a good highdeea. Lee me alone for a bid.

Nut Take him through it, Rock. *Rock moves into the chair opposite Billy's and holds his hands. To Jacky.* Keep still. Let them work it out, or your boy will flip the lid. OK Carstairs?
Bull holds his fists, threatening Jacky.

Rock *Sings.* I seen California dreaming, with those flowers in their hair...

Billy *Looks up at Rock and tightens the hand hold, sings.* Roses are red my love, Roses are blue. Just the... Just the,

Rock Golden light.

Billy Sand and sea. *Drops his head.*

Rock Blue light and sleeping and floating, in the air.

Billy *Looks up.* Roses in the air.

Rock Yeah man, and wind softly over roses.

Billy There's a tree...

Rock Yeah. Yeah. Go. Go.

Billy A tree. White tree. And I'm smiling. That's me laughing, man. See me laughing.

Rock Yeah. You're great man. That's fine.

Billy And some..

Rock White birds of paradise. Yeah?

Billy Oh, yeah. Folding in and out, man. Like white married with light. *Laughs in pleasure.*

Rock You're good, man. You're seeing. Call them, man. Like in your own language. *Billy calls in a forgotten, strange tongue.* Stay, beneath the tree. With the white birds. We're together, man. Hold. Like, love, man. Like peace. *Rock and Billy smile at each other and increase their hold into a firm tight grip. Rock nods to Nut.* OK, Nut.

Nut *To Jacky.* Rock can take him in any direction. Give him the roller coaster to hell. So listen. Listen.

Rock You are in the banana trees. All yellow.

Billy Like the sun. *Sings*. Yellow bird high up in banana tree.

Rock *Looks at manager, back to Billy.* You got away from this dirty world, right?

Billy No dirt, please, dark cupboards under the stairs, tight, dirty. Help me! The walls are on my face, man!

Rock *Looks at the shocked Manager and smiles, holds Billy's head*. Easy, Bill. Easy in it. *Rock and Billy sing, a made up rock number.* Freedom, through the universe.

Billy At peace, man. Yeah, at peace. I can see my innocent baby's world, and all the colours of the universe.

Luigi Nize song, Billy.

Jacky What have you nutcases done? You bloody idiots!

Billy No! No! Dirty faces, red faces, ugly faces, cuts, cuts and slicing, split my eyes! Help me! Help me! Help me!

Rock *To manager.* Shut up you swinging London poof! *Resumes the song*. Peaceful waters of the universe.

Luigi Uh? Uh?

Nut Luigi...

Luigi Issa worst dan der blutty blagshirds, mun, or der

brownshirds or der bustard Klew Klun Klan. Loog ad him for Chrissake! *Stares at Nut.* What ew done, eh? What ew done, eh? What ew done, mun! Issa real crime habbening yer now, mun!

Nut *Nastily.* Yeah, Luigi. This is the second crime. First crime you saw was when they smashed you in nineteen forty.

Jacky Is this a bloody mental institution? You're all flaming 'eaders. You're all sick men. You get some perverted pleasure from all this? You dropped acid on Billy. Christ, how much did you drop? Uh? You could change his personality, mess his career up! You headbangers.

Nut Lips. Shut them, lovely heart.

Jacky What are you, uh? Sick kids? Wobblies? Uh? What you want, man? Today is supposed to be a sad day, the great hero, the big procession.

Nut Quiet now, Lips. Listen, cockney twang rat. I'm the manager OK?

Bull What manager, Nut?

Nut I just thought of it, right! Manager of the underground world champs. Look at this. *Produces a paper.* Horror scope, OK. In the paper. "Don't think the world is against you. Go out and think positive. You are, I am, whatever you want to be. You are the centre of the world. You are a bundle of possibilities. Live one day at a time" I can understand that,

OK cocky? I went to Grammar School. I passed. But they couldn't afford the bastard gym kit, right? You might laugh! You either sink or swim, OK? And this, look at this, London flab. *Produces an old newspaper cutting. To Luigi and Bull.* Who's that, boys?

Bull A little boy.

Luigi Iss a small kidt.

Nut It's me, you crams. Listen. "Young and business-like, eleven-year-old Rodney Chang..."

Bull *Collapses.* Who's that ?

Nut Me, you cred. "..is ambitious for a youngster, and organised and enthusiastic with it. Little Rodney is seen here selling old comics on a stand of his own invention. Rodney tells us he made it from an orange box and two Brillo packets. Just what we need in the Valleys, young initiative. Good luck and God bless you Rodney!"

Bull More. Read more.

Nut Nothing more you idjits. What's this..." Jacky Mahoney hid the axe in his mother's coat.." No, that's the court news. Anyway, London, listen. The boys lost their licence, OK? Naughty boys, OK? Boys will be boys. We got. My champs for that ugly dirty outside, am I right?

Billy No black, dirty, please, tunnels. I can see death! Ahh! Death!

Rock *Shouts him down with the song.* Ooooh! Yeah! Yeah! Cool waters of the universe.

Jacky I'll get the cops on this. You'll swing for this.

Rock Swing, swing, through the banana trees. *Billy is peaceful, eyes closed.*

Nut *Putting his arm around the Manager.* Listen Queenie. Billy's on acid, right? The cops are big on drugs down here, right? We'll say you brought the acid. Right? Peddling drugs from London. Simple. Who they going to believe? And during the hero's funeral. Bad. Really bad, Westminster. *To Luigi.* Billy Sticks or shut your mouth. No protection, OK, Pomeroni Spaghetti?

Luigi Bill stigs, no. He buss my door.

Nut Alright, alright! No Billy Sticks. Get your phone. *To Bull.* Take the London pimp out the back. *To Jacky.* OK, London boy? You goes with Bull, you phone the papers, you ask for the top sports guy, you tell them about us. They'll listen because, you're a famous fart, see? Twangy! Billy Dreamer stays with us, to have another little dream or maybe ten more little tabs.

Jacky When do I take Billy? Christ, this is so flaming crazy!

Nut After. That's the li'l ole deal. After. And listen. This is it, right? You want a big feature, OK? You've seen the two best fighters you've ever seen. Tops, right? Tops! Better than America. You tell the papers about how good we are. And the names, right? Bull, Rock and Nut, the greatest team. Bull, Rock and Nut could have been great, right? *To Bull.* You go with cockney sweetie.

Bull *Shadow boxing on his way to the side room with Jacky.* Marciano, tramp! Maxie Baer, sump! Jacky Johnson, crack! Johnny Weissmuller, stamp! Flash Gordon, Jusp! Cassius Clay, huss! Billy Sticks, snap! George Horse...

Luigi High thingk high ged oud of all dis. Go back to Italy. They say, welcome back Luigi. Where you bin? Loog ad all der grabe fields thad grow when you had gone away. *Exits shaking his head.*

Rock *In the direction of the kitchen door, in a Dean Martin style.* But I'm the Prince, who takes the King, remember that, remember this. *Rising, posing, the superstar.* I'm the Prince of the town, I'll take the King, I'll take the King's crown!
Rock returns to sway with Billy. Nut arranges three chairs in a row.

Nut Rock! Close him up.

Rock *Folds Billy's arm around his head.* Sleep a baby. Ohhh, Hmmm, hmmmm.

Nut Rock. Get ready for take-off, baby.
Nut sits Rock down on one of the end chairs. Luigi, Manager and Bull return.

Jacky I don't know what you expect from a little tarting local paper.

Nut Ah, shut up. Luigi, did he talk ?

Luigi He talked alright. You could be famous now.

Nut Bull! Sit yer. Photograph, Bull. Famous boxer. *Sits Bull down at the other end. Jacky attempts to wake the doped Billy. Waving to fans in arrogant confidence.* They chair poets,right? Top athletes, right? *Sits in the middle chair..*

Jacky *With a semi comatose, singing Billy.* You crazy nutters. I'll be back. I'll see you straight. What a bum place. You yokel idiots. I can cancel that newspaper story, you'll see.

Nut *Waves him away without turning his head.* Live one day at a time, boy!

Bull Could a dog fight a fox?

Jacky *Opens the door, the rough tough East Ender.* What's this uh? This cheap filthy dump, this pigshit, this nowhere shack? You two-penny-halfpenny crocks! I'll be back with muscle that'll crack your guts, take you apart, spread you all over this hill-billy nannygoat craphill! You wait for it, I'll put this thing on! I'll make you scream! I'll make you wish you'd never seen me in your stinking little lives!

Luigi Jaggy mun, today is a sad...

Jacky You clown. You idiot clown. You'd better wish you'd stayed with the eye-ties in Greasyland! You fucking creeping Jesus, I'll have your Roman cock kicked off! *Holding Billy with one hand he points at the tableau, teeth bared.* Scum rats! Blood cunts! Piss Welshies! *Spits on the floor.* Go take a bath!

Billy *Holds Jacky's face and sings.* Peaceful waters of the universe.

Jacky Fuck off, chocolate cake, or I'll put you back in the fucking swamp where you belong!

Luigi *Walking to the door.* Uh? you get outa my place. Idiots indeed. Dun yew come yer! Good Godt was ey thing ey sayin! *Pushes them out and closes the door.* Pizz off! Smazzin my houze, smazzin my farder. You godt to fight der bastards bag! *Walks to Nut, who has risen.* Mebbe I shoulda fought hadder den.

Nut Yeah, you should have Luigi, but... *Shakes head.* Nineteen Forty, Luigi. You're still on the wireless. This is now kid. We're fighting now.

Luigi Dun hurd everybody, Nud. Nor me, Nud.

Nut Everybody, Luigi. Everybody who dragged us in the bullshit.

Luigi Dun be a blagshird, fightding in der streeds.

Nut Just fighting back, Luigi. You know. Last time.

Luigi Lass time ever, Nud?

Nut Last time ever, Luigi. We're dead. We're gone.

Luigi Tara, Nud. *They shake hands.* You funny boys, ai! Dun hurd innocent people, though.

Nut We fought back Luigi. Last time. You won't see us again. It could have... *In imitation...* bin anybuddy in yer today, mun.

Luigi *Laughs.* You funny boys, ai!

Nut They needed you in Italy a long time ago, Luigi.
Nut returns to his seat, a study in learnt helplessness.

Luigi I dun know, Nud. *Points to the floor, meaning the cafe.* Free country in it mun. *Looks at his watch, gets on with things.* Doo o'glock. Star's open boys!

Bull, Rock, and Nut 1983. Robert Blythe, Ray Handy, Roger Nott, Terry Jackson, Dorien Thomas. Photo: Ian Lawrence

Design: Simon Banham

IN SUNSHINE
AND IN SHADOW
a new play
by ALAN OSBORNE
SHERMAN
ARENA
CARDIFF
Tues–Sat
19–23 November, 8pm
Tickets £3.70 & £2.70
(reductions exc. Sat)
Box Office 0222 30451
MADE IN
WALES

IN SUNSHINE AND IN SHADOW

A situation tragedy

In Sunshine and In Shadow was first performed by Made In Wales Stage Company at the Sherman Theatre in 1985 with the following cast

VEE	Di Botcher
DAY	Terry Jackson
BABES	Theresa Hennessey
GA-GA	Phil Babot
PIXIE*	Peter Richards
CISSIE	William Ingram
STACK	Robert Blythe
BERNIE	Stephen Botcher
DAI DEATH	Ray Handy

directed by **Gareth Armstrong**
designed by **Richard Alwyn**
project director **Gilly Adams**

This version was performed by the Merthyr Inc. at Battersea Arts Centre in 1992.

with Steve Botcher, Terry Dauncey, Rhodri Huw, John North & Shelley Rees
Directed by Dorien Thomas

*Pixie did not make the final cut

Set

The three main walls display a collage of famous images. The back wall has a black, empty fire-grate hole in a central position (no heater, no tiles), an old settee at back stage left; there is a door at back stage right. This door opens onto a kitchenette. Images may be seen on the walls, a table and chair may be seen.There is another door, front stage left - this leads to the main front door and the hallway may be glimpsed. The main room floor is covered with a fitted, threadbare red carpet. A white bed has faded white accessories with added bows and frills - genteel, but almost with doll's house associations. The headboard is a white plastic reproduction of ornate filigree, and positioned onto the right stage wall. Behind the bed is a large drape which partly obscures the wall - this is referred to as the 'secret'. At the near bedside is a cabinet which contains a radio and a cassette player and a green slops bucket. The bedside has a hard-backed chair; another hard-backed chair is positioned in centre stage - on this chair is positioned a tailor's dummy with moveable joints. The dummy points upwards to the ceiling - which we can only presume to be saturated with Michelangelo's 'Last Judgement'.

It would be necessary for this environment to contain a part of the external environment, and that is, to contain the red monumental word Kong's high above the set. We would assume that the top half of the house is transparent.

One small, very dim, naked electric light bulb lights the scene.

In Sunshine

Two men are inspecting a load of building equipment. This equipment is piled loosely outside a boarded up council house. Hardboard and plaster-board sheets, shovels, bags of plaster, nail-box, large paint cans, brushes, step ladder, bag of tools, crow-bars. A sign states that this is Bloomsbury Crescent. The men are council workers. Stack, the elder, is nearing sixty, a large powerful build - he wears a blue council tunic with his shirt open at the neck. The other man is Bernie, dressed in a council tunic with white tee-shirt He has a shaven head - about early twenties, signs of tattoos on his arms. A third person, Gareth, to whom they occasionally refer is out of view.

The boarded up house has adolescent insignia sprayed on the boards in large letters - Beaky, Shagg, Dando, Grum, Dunjun. A crude drawing of a dagger slices downward through a human skull, and drips with red blood.

Kim Davies Loves Gutsy
Kim Davies Loves Sharky
Kim Davies has been eaten

It is Summer. Late Morning. May/June.

Stack *Lights his pipe and stares front.*

Bernie *Checks through the provisions and equipment.*
Candles? O! Right.

Stack *Without turning* White primer in, Bernie?

Bernie Yeah, white primer in, Stacky, and the petrol's in.

Stack Formosan Seas.

Bernie Where?

Stack Out there. *Bernie joins Stack and stares into the distance.* We used to pick illegal immigrants from Formosa and drop 'em on the Chinese mainland. Genoa as well, Genoa to Haifa, all the European refugees. They'll come out now, out of the trees, out of the ground, just appear. Bright sunny days, just like today. Coast clear for miles. Then, boop! All appear. Look!

Bernie O yeah, kids, look. Where did those miligrunts come from, Stacky?

Stack I don't know, Bernie. I wasn't there to think, orders were to pick 'em up like, so pick 'em up we did. In those days, Bernie, you just obeyed. Look. Over there, over there, over there. All shapes and sizes.

Bernie They coming here, Stacky?

Stack Only too right they are. I'm expecting a big crowd. Day one, Bernie. Curious see. Where's Gareth ?

Bernie Gareth! He must be deaf. *Laugh* Hear that, Stacky? He must be deaf!

Stack Laugh as far as the crow bar, Bernie. And laugh down those boards on the door.

Bernie Jesus! There's going to be hundreds here in a minute, Stacky. *Turns and finds a bar. Pulls on the boards, continually looking at the growing crowd.* Stacky?

Stack What ?

Bernie How come this door is blue and all the other houses are orange? This place has been untouched.

Stack *Taps out his pipe, turns, seizes bar and proceeds to remove boards on the side of the house.* Day one, Bernie. Move! Move!

Bernie *Tugging* Ghost town, Stacky. Masters of the universe !

Stack Gareth! *points to side of stage* I can see you, boy! I can see you.

Bernie You going to smack him one in the mouth, Mr.Stack? *Faces the crowd. Points.* Hop it, kid! He only got one leg, Stacky! Mr. Stack, you er, still like, haven't said why we come. What we doing, Mr.Stack? Union squabble is it?

Stack Put those boards, nails pointing up, around. Stop the natives charging the gangplank. *Produces a piece of paper from his top pocket.* Bernie. Read it.

Bernie *Reading* Bloomsbury Crescent? Double suicide?

Stack *Plucks the paper from Bernie* That's enough, Dogsbreath.

Bernie I was just reading what happened to the two kids.

Stack Put 'em in care, Bernie, split 'em, put 'em in care, like they do. *Looks in Gareth's direction.* We had a fella, Curly Sullivan. The fella was O.K. Good worker, Cardiff boy. Strong as an ox. In those days, Bernie, they used the Queen's docks for cold storage. American coffins jammed tight. Curly Sullivan refused to go in. *Nods* He reminds me of Curly.

Bernie Big fella as well?

Stack Ai, disobeyed orders, slapped him in irons, put him inside. *Points to Gareth* You'll be the next to go inside, kid. Mark my words.

Bernie You told me in the truck it was all salvage, Mr.Stack, salvage work back then.

Stack That's right, Bernie. Panamanian, Swedish, British, Danish, Liberian to name but a few, my friend

Bernie Er! What a stink, Stacky. Er! Pitch black in there, Stacky.

Stack Pass those two primer cans, Bernie. Sit down, Bernie. Don't look at the audience, kid. Look at me. Look at me, Bernie!

Act relaxed! *Lights his pipe* Do what I'm telling you, sharpish. Don't look at the audience, right?

Bernie Right, Stacky.

Stack Don't look at them, Bernie. Don't look. Ai, we brought the old battle-wagon, The Iron Duke, down from Tankerness. Admiral Jellicoe's flag ship. Don't look, Bernie. As I was saying, they had Admiral Jellicoe's uniform, all preserved in the after-quarters, under glass, the whole dress uniform and sword, like...

Bernie You see it, Stacky?

Stack I disobey orders, Bernie. *Looks at open door.* We'll let the stink out, Bernie. Let it breathe see, kid. Let a bit of sunshine in. I can smell it from here. Bernie, look at me, my friend. They, er, they beginning to move?

Bernie *Sneaks a glance* A lot of 'em are moving away, Stacky.

Stack Ai. I thought they would. Soon as you open the door. Anyway, look at me, Bernie. As you were saying, not a union squabble, collaboration between councils, local council won't go in. People are unwilling to live in these houses. Local council will do the outside rendering, tarting it up a bit. We do the inside. People don't realise, Bernie - what life is on these giant estates. Biggest estate in Europe this. I couldn't live here. I'd go barmy.

Bernie Tell you what though, Stacky.

Stack ?

Bernie They got out of it!

Stack O'yeah, boy. They got out of it alright.You got the candles.

Bernie Any light in there, then?

Stack No light.

Bernie Jesus wept - how can I plaster by candlelight?

Stack Bernie. Listen, day one right. We take out some wall panels, wallpaper and ceiling plaster boards. Three rooms only. Three of us. Clear? Day two, we fix in new panels, day three, plaster and paint. I've been over and over it in the office. Day one, *finger sprouts up,* take out all existing ceiling board, some panels. Some wallpaper in lounge, dining room, in kitchenette, *drops his finger* burn them.

Bernie Burn them!

Stack Outside on the front garden, if you can call it a garden, burn them. That's why we got the petrol, my friend. Day two. New stuff, already piled inside, put it up.

Bernie What's he doing then?
Turns and nods to Gareth off stage.

Stack After day one, Gareth will be painting the hallway, *on his fingers, counting* landing, bathroom, boxroom, two bedrooms, white primer, day three and four he paints kitchenette, diner and lounge – white.

Bernie All white!

Stack All white.

Bernie All white inside, fires in the garden.
Shakes head in disbelief

Stack Right first time, Bernie!

Bernie *Head shaking again.* Plaster won't be dry.

Stack Forget it. Orders are, paint it ! Over the weekend on special overtime, local council to take down boards off windows and doors. Everything patched up outside. Alright Bernie, not by us, by them.

Bernie What we doing about the house next door?

Stack Nothing wrong with it, perfect. *Pauses and squints at Bernie* Would you like to live next door to a haunted house? *Looks at his watch.* Go and tell Curly Sullivan to look after the place. We'll have a couple of hours of a liquid lunch, Bernie Boy. *Looks at the open, dark door.* Let the stink out. *Walks to the stage right.Without turning.* Don't look at them, Bernie!

Bernie Don't worry you, all this, Mr.Stack.

Stack *Lights his pipe* Nothing like this worries me, my friend. That's why they appointed me. When I'm on a salvage job, I'm a law unto myself. Obey orders, Bernie! Day one.
They exit

SCENE I

The skin of the external set is cast off. Inside there is a room and a bed. A lady sits up, looking in a mirror.

Vee Day.... Day... Day! *pause* Day! .... Day! .... Day! *Turns to the sleeping figure.* Day!

Day I'll be there now. I'm buying a car.

Vee Don't have a coma on me, Day, please! It's a coma.. Good God, a beautiful day in summer. And he's having a coma on me!

Day Leave it there, Vee. Leave it there, love. Pain on entry, Vee. Dried up, Vee. Pain on entry, Vee.

Vee Oh yeah! You need sugar, alright. You need sugar, Day? Get up and fill your St. Pancreas with Tate and Lyle, Day!
The man hoists himself up, turns and sits on the bed edge. He wears a pair of briefs. His clothes are scattered beneath his feet and on the hard-backed chair.

Day Had your black and greens,Vee?

Vee What you mean, you bad bugger?

Day Get the tablets down you, love!

Vee You cheeky swine!

Day Don't do the nerves, Vee!

Vee I wouldn't go to you even if I had thirty palpitation attacks!

Day Don't be childish, Vee.

Vee Get to work, you big get. Lucky bastard, you can get out of it!

Day *Dressing*. Get out of it! Get out of it!

Vee You're talking double, Day. You need sugar!

Day I need nothing, cow.

Vee Sugar, Day. *Leans back. Lights a cigarette. Day continues dressing*. Pass the bucket, I'm busting. Pass the bucket! *Watches him*. Pass the bucket, Day? Come on, love.

Day No bucket, no tablets, no nothing, no club!

Vee You're a bad bugger, you are! *Day is searching for a coat around the room. She claps her hands twice. Clap-clap. Clap-*

clap. Ga-Ga! *Clap-clap*, Ga-Ga! *Day stops the search and imitates in mime the clapping.*What do you mean, Day? What do you mean? What's the look for, Day? What's the look for?

Day Leave it there, Vee!

Vee No, Day. What's the look for? *Day finds his coat. Puts it on. He walks to the dummy and curtly smacks the face.*

Vee Me isn't it, Day? You diabetic swine! *Crawls back into bed, staring. Day pushing the dummy off the chair, sits, rolls up the trouser leg. Takes an insulin pack from his coat pocket, produces a needle, fills it with insulin from a small container, finds a spot and injects.* You diabetic get!

Day *Drawing out the needle slowly.* Still scared of the dark, Vee?

Vee Call yourself a man, do you ? Big man in the club last night. Nothing big man wouldn't do. You coward, Day. You beater! See the yellow streak on his back. A man ? Don't make me sick! *Day injection completed, rolls down his trouser leg.* You ignorant swine. You diabetic get.

Day Dullest girl in Wales ! Dullest girl in Wales ! Gerr-up ! *He batters the table as a drum.* Get up. *Stands at the door.* I must have seen thirty people last night in the club.

Vee Corny swines.

Day Yes, Vee, thirty people, all said the same, Vee, know what they said, Vee?

Vee I couldn't care less, I hate them and you!

Day Thirty people. What she doing singing in this dump? There you are, Vee, what you doing singing in that dump? Thirty people. She could be on the stage, that girl.

Vee Who said that?

Day Thirty people, Vee, thirty people!

Vee Who cares a shit anyway. It's only a hole of a place.

Day Don't be a big head, Vee.

Vee Quick! Ooh! Pass the bucket love, quick! Pass the bucket, you swine! Come on!

Day Little kiss first.

Vee Quick then! *Day walks to Vee slowly. They kiss, she breaks.* Hmm ! Pass the bucket, love. *Day to the cupboard, takes out the green bucket, brings it to Vee. Vee rises out, sits on the bucket.*

Day *Going to kitchen.* Pixie-face.

Vee What he say? Pixie-face?

Day *Buttering bread.* They're going to arrest you.

Vee Arrest me? For what?

Day Not sending the children to school.

Vee What about you, then? Debtors' prison! And you listened to him, Pixie-face, 'cos I wouldn't give him this much. *Fingers indicate a small size.* You must be demented, listening to Pixie-face, like that old cow next door, big Myfanwy mouth, they're as thick as thieves. Yap! Yap! Yap! You'll be telling me next to have Ga-Ga put back in care! I'm right, aren't I? Huh? You'll have to kill me first before I send him back!

Day *Shows her the knife menacingly.* I'll take him back, leave it to me!

Vee Take him back. *Rises, pulls down her night-dress.* Why should I take him back? My own flesh and blood. You'll get me demented. *Back into bed. Silence. Day wraps the bread in a newspaper.* You want that though, don't you? *Day places the packet in his pocket.* Look at me!

Day Look at you!

Vee I struggled my guts out, irons on my legs.

Day I bet you struggled your guts out with iron on your legs.

Vee Carried me everywhere as a child.

Day I bet they carried you everywhere.

Vee I wasn't put away! Lame I was.

Day Those were the days when you were lame, Vee. *Vee holds two fingers in a 'V' sign.* You had your own way, a spoilt little cow, a spoilt little cow. *Repetitive, a chant beneath his breath.*

Vee Spoilt, I'm sure, if I was spoilt I wouldn't be a prisoner on this estate, I wouldn't have Myfanwy mouth next door. I'd be out of it, boy!

Day You nutter!

Vee Nutter? If I'm a nutter you put me there!

Day Stupid nutter!

Vee I'm not having him put back! You put him back and I'm off!

Day I'm coming in, Vee. Playing thieves, Vee. Thieves in the night, Vee, not going to work, Vee. Thieves. *Grabs her neck beneath the covers.* This is it, Vee. The big one. Chokey-chokey. A million pounds, Vee. How you going to spend it ?

Vee Cancer research. Half a million. And get your head tested the other half !
They both laugh.

Day I'd spend it on your voice. Get it trained properly. Smashing clothes. Say so-long to this dump.

Vee You'd piss it up against the wall, you liar.

Day *Thoughtfully.* You're a whore.

Vee I beg your pardon!

Day Nothing.

Vee I'm a what? A what, Day?

Day Nothing.

Vee A what? A whore? You sugar-faced swine, get off!

Day I'm off, whorey, bye, whorey, bye bye, dullsy batsy. *Walks to the stage door left. Twiddles his fingers in a ta-ta gesture.* Bye, whorey. *Both hold each other in a long drawn out battle stare.*

Vee What you're trying to say, Day, is that you don't want caviar for dinner tonight? And, let me read your mind slowly right? Please Vee, will you press my best top hat and tails.

Day Whore!

Vee Wait a minute sweetie, I'm getting the message through, we'll dance till dawn down the boulevard? *Day walks to the dummy. Picks it up aggressively by the neck.* Yes, go on. Ga-Ga's dummy. *Day points at the ceiling* Yes, the last judgement. *Day points at the drape.*Yes, the secret. *Day points at the walls.* All the pictures, yes? You want them out, out!

Day Out! Burned! *Throws down the dummy. Marches to the door.* You'll get us evicted, you'll turn the boy homo. *He hits the door*. Burned! Burned! Out! Burned! *He exits still banging the cheap walls of the house.* Burned! *The pounding is ceaseless. Myfanwy starts to rise against the pounding. The pounding ceases. Myfanwy is loud.*

Vee *Stands on the bed and hammers the wall.* O.K. Myfanwy! OK! We've got the message! We heard it thirty times yesterday! *Myfanwy ceases abruptly. Vee sits on the bed and lights a cigarette stub.*

SCENE II

Vee sobs quietly, she sighs deeply and rests her head on the headboard and looks at the ceiling. She closes her eyes, stillness. A girl appears in the stage door left entrance. Softly, ghostly she moves to the gap between the curtains, and opens it slightly more. The strong shaft of light is like a stage spotlight. This child has a short beaver lamb coat across her shoulders, a white night-dress, dirty feet in high heels, and face bruised, wearing cheap national health glasses. She softly twirls in a dance figure. She poses in crude swan like movements.

Vee Jesus, I've got another beauty here! *wipes her eyes and watches the small performance.* Hey, Babes, do this! *Vee makes* *more sophisticated gestures with her arms. Babes copies* That's good.

Babes *Sits on the bed smiling.* Mam, can I wear these. If I goes on a message?

Vee You can't go on a message like that. *Thinks, silence.* Yeah, why not! Stand up! *Babes does this quickly.* Christ, to think I wore that to marry that swine at sixteen.

Babes You said fifteen, before.

Vee Liar! I carried Ga-Ga at fifteen and a half. We got married at sixteen. I wanted it white, without a sickly baby screaming. Go check the window for him.

Babes *Dutifully goes.* No one there, mam, he's gone away.

Vee Come here! Message to Cissie. Gimmie a pencil. *Babes goes beneath the bed.* Come on or I'll forget it! *Babes produces a pencil stub. Gives the pencil to Vee and dances away lightly.* Pass that brown paper bag under the settee. *Babes dances to the settee and locates the bag. Dances back, using the paper as part of her act. Sits on bed. Vee snatches the paper and attempts to write. She continually licks the pencil stub.* Shit! *Turns the paper over.* What's this?

Babes A star for school.

Vee A star ? X that is. *Draws it in the air with her finger.*

Pointing at Babes. That's the last time you'll go there!

Babes I got to go before Christmas. The school party, Mam.

Vee School party! They don't have 'em anymore!

Babes Mandy said they do.

Vee Yeah! And Mandy was smoking at five. And her mother's carrying on, the cow! *Turns the paper again and tries to write.*

Babes Mam? When was your first singing contest ?

Vee *Stops writing.* I told you yesterday. *Loud.* I went to Swansea! *Softening.* Cissie had you and Ga-Ga. *Softening more and leaning back looking at the ceiling.* It was lovely, ai... Me and your father... He wasn't sugar then...Shoulda seen the place, Babes. All white, you know, with like brass lights. There was hundreds there, hundreds, I nearly died when they called me, and all those lights, in your face. I won easy!

Babes What did you win?

Vee Nothing, the swines! I had to go to Bimbos in Torquay, for the semi-finals. But that jealous man wouldn't let me go, know what he called me? *Looking at the ceiling.* Like that Devil up there he is! Same ugly face!

Babes *Looking up, pointing.* That Jesus looks like Dad.

Vee No, he don't. The devil do! hey! Shut up, you silly cow. I'm sure you got sugar like him! *Pauses, licks the pencil, thinks, leans back.* When I done the clubs, right, I won in the 'Castle' with a ballad. In the 'Temp' I was robbed, I've done.. *On her fingers counting.* The Palace, Lyceum, Road to London. *On the other hand counting.* Glamourous mother.. first. Queen of Hearts, first. Minkie's Club, first. Second Chance, first. Fountain Club for two nights. Why don't you come back, Vee ? Hanging on me, they were! Talk of the Town, first. Red Cow, the cows. Never even asked me. Martyr's club, won it hands down! *She looks at the paper and reflects. Shakes her head.* Take this message to Cissie! *Begins to write.* How do you spell wages?

Babes Wear-jis.

Vee Spell it mun!

Babes W-E-J-I-Z. *Closes her eyes and spells each letter phonetically.*

Vee *Writing.* That don't look right you illiterate swine! *Cuffs Babes across the head. Attempts to write again with loud difficulty. Babes sucks her thumb loudly. Without looking up.* Shut up! I'm concentrating! *Vee lands a second smack.* Take your thumb out or I'll batter you! Clean the bucket out! Get my moggies!

Babes *Picks up the slop bucket. Stops. Studies her hand.* What's all these red circles, Mam ?

Vee Red circles ? What red circles ?

Babes I got 'em all over itching.

Vee Show me. *Looks.* Heat bumps.

Babes And in my mouth ?

Vee Heat bumps, call Ga-Ga.

Babes Ga-Ga. *Thump-thump on bucket.* Ga-Ga! Any breakfast, mam?

Vee Breakfast! Like hell you'll have breakfast, you lazy swine, you haven't done a stroke of work yet!

Babes *Marching as a drummer, beating the bucket.* Ga-Ga! Ga-Ga! Ga-Ga!

Vee Shut up! *A knock at the door. Freezes. Quietly.* Listen. *Babes appears, treading softly.* It's the doctor. *Furiously wipes off her make-up in the bed sheet. Scuffs her hair, snuggles down in bed.* Open it, Babes.

Babes *Disappears to open the main front door. Silence. Runs back to Vee and in a loud whisper.* I don't know who he is .

Vee *Through clenched teeth.* Ask him who he is then.

Babes *Trips to the door quickly.* Wait a minute. *Runs back to Vee.*

Vee *Stops Babes half-way.* Get back, you nutter! *Babes turns.* Has he got a slouch hat? Funny pop eyes?

Babes I don't know.

Vee Pissing hell, get back! Tell him my mother's dead! We're going to the funeral!

Babes *To the doorway again.* Yes, yes, yes. My mother's dead. *Vee pulls at her hair and falls backwards.* Yes, yes, it's my coat. So long.

Vee *Beside herself with temper.* Come here! Come here, you nutter! *Vee is out of bed. Babes runs and hides behind the settee.* Come yuh! Come yuh! *Vee picks up the slops bucket and tips it behind the settee.* I'm sure you got sugar! *Walks to the slit in the curtains, peers out like a thief.* It was the rent man, the bastard! Look at him walking, the suck arse, yeah, with the council behind him, he's the hard man with cripples and lonely spastic women. *Places the bucket back in the cupboard. She moves back to bed, flinging and banging, huffing and puffing. Lights a cigarette stub, inhales deeply. Starts her make up all over again, ashtray on the bed.* Wait till I tell your father, he'll beat seventeen different colours of shit out of you! *Resumes the work on her face. Babes rises, wet hair, glasses askew.*You are, right, and you look, right, the dullest girl in Wales! Get out of there. See if woman beater is gone.

Babes *To the window, walking cautiously. Glasses still askew. Looks out of the slit, up and down, up and down. Closes the* *curtains with a tug.* There's a car outside with flashing lights.

Vee Uh? Where? *Rises and runs to the window.* Where? I can't see a car with flashing lights. *She looks up.* It's the flaming sun, you stupid girl!

Babes Ambulance.

Vee Sun, stupid! *Bumps Babes' head with her hand. Goes back to bed. Babes is a forlorn statue.*

Babes Mammy ?

Vee You'd be glad if I done myself in. *Rummages for something.*

Babes Mammy, mun ?

Vee It's like Casey's Court in here.

Babes Mam !

Vee *Stops the search, looks at Babes.* What's the look for? Ai like Ding. You'll take off that beaver lamb !

Babes But Mammy, mun !

Vee What !

Babes I'm wet all over.

Vee I'll wet you now, in a minute. Go on a message to Kong's for fags. Say I'll pay him tonight when your father comes home.

Babes What fags, Mam?

Vee Gold ones, sixty.

Babes *To the door submissively.* What'll happen if they haven't got gold ones?

Vee Red ones!

Babes *Opens the door.* What'll happen if they haven't got red ones?

Vee Black ones!

Babes What'll happen if they haven't got black ones, Mam?

Vee Get out! Bring me anything! *Babes goes out, slams the door. Vee settles with her mirror and studies her eyes.*

Babes *Gently tapping the window.* Mammy, Mammy.

Vee What's that ?

Babes Me, Mammy.

Vee Jesus Christ! I'll brain you, I will! You're causing blue murder you are!

Babes Mammy, I haven't got shoes on.

Vee Shoes on! Shoes on! I'll give you shoes on! *She rises out of bed, searches, finds a pair of large wellingtons. Opens the window.* Yuh! *Throws them out. The emotion has stiffened her, she stands and holds her head. She looks at the ceiling,spits,goes to the kitchen and returns swallowing tablets from a medicine bottle. Re-enters her bed and claps her hands. Clap-clap.* Ga-Ga! *Clap-clap.* Ga-Ga *Clap-clap.* Ga-Ga!

She waits, no response, looks through her bag, finds an old photograph. Unfolds it. Stares and leans back on her pillow. Sobs. Wipes her eyes. Sings with passion.

But come ye back
When spring is on the meadow
And da da da, da dum.
And white with snow
And I'll be there
In sunshine and in shadow.

Enter Ga-Ga. Slouches to the white drape and looks behind it.

Ga-Ga Hmm. Hmm. Hmm ?

Vee Honest to God. Baby's life. No-one's looked. *Claps her hands to the words. Clap. Clap. Clap.* No-one's looked. *Ga-Ga goes behind the curtains. Babes enters.*Get the fags? *Sudden change of tone. Babes holds a carrier bag and fiddles with the handles nervously.* Come on, gimme the fags! *Pauses.* What you got there?

Babes *Puts in her hand and pulls out a packet.* Ajax.

Vee Who gave you Ajax?

Babes With a wire brush. *Pulls out the brush.*

Vee Ajax and a wire brush? Ajax ? Ajax ?

Babes You said to bring ...

Vee Not Ajax.... fags!

Babes Anything.

Vee What?

Babes You said bring anything.

Vee *Swoons backwards holding her heart, and through clenched teeth in a mock attack.* Go and ask Pixie Face for fags. Tell Cissie to come. *Babes runs off quickly. Enter Ga-Ga. Smiles and goes for Vee like a beast. Vee screams and burrows down beneath the blankets. Ga-Ga makes circle movements in the air.* What's that, then? *Clap! Clap! Clap!* What's that, then?

Ga-Ga Hmm...Hmm.

Vee Who? *Ga-Ga hands Vee a torn picture. Vee studies it.*

Ga-Ga *Points at picture.* Hmm.. Hmm.

Vee O yeah. Good God. O yeah. Lenard Hardy. *Closer look.* Len...ardo...der...vink...high! *Looks up at Ga-Ga. Claps her hands. Clap! Clap!* Lenard Hardy! *Ga-Ga, pleased, dances and paints the air. Myfanwy breaks through softly.* Alright love, alright. Get back in and finish my birthday painting. You got till tomorrow to finish the secret. Go back! *Ga-Ga picks up his picture, waltzes back behind the curtain. Myfanwy louder. Vee stands on the bed and hammers the wall.* Will you give it a rest ! *Myfanwy's speed increases and then ceases abruptly. Vee lies back and looks at the ceiling.* We're all on a slippery slope downhill. They'll put a plaque on the door. Fifteen quid entrance fee to see the paintings. Everything else will be flat, black, collapsed, thirty thousand boxes, dust and ashes. Vee-Ronica Bernadette not Boulevard, a shop. "The Colouring Box". Teas, coffee, ices. Like a flag stuck in an arsehole. *Sings dramatically* Till all the seas run dry ! *Ga-Ga emerges.* Do you ever get that feeling that you're living behind a veil thing. Like a piece of fluff floating in the air ? *Lies back.* Phenomogitrons I'm on as well. In the hospital there was a gold angel. And the nurse, a gold nurse. She took him off me, and her hands were gold colour. *Stares at Ga-Ga, he stares back.* I'm talking about your brother. You understand, don't you? There's something going to happen, isn't it? You know, don't you? The nurse said she'd see me again. *She stares, transfixed by Ga-ga. Ga-Ga goes to the kitchen door and turns, stares at Vee and walks threateningly, holding an imaginary baby cradled in his arms. Frightened.* You know, don't you, you know. *Ga-Ga holds out his arms. His very silence and disability makes him a haunted figure. Babes appears stage door left. In wedding dress and a posy of cigarettes. One hand balances a book on her head, like a crown.* What do you think in there? *Points to her head.* You know, don't you. *Ga-ga places the imaginary shape next to Vee and lies down. Vee hugs and kisses him. Babes walks slowly, as in a procession, stopping and curtsying.* Know what I'd really like. To be able to walk down the street, never scared, catch a train and don't shake with panic. Go on a journey and not crash. I could go to Harley Street or a big American clinic. Nerves is a thing of the past out there. I could buy the best drugs. Red and silvers, blue and gold. Diamond drugs. See me, you know,. li'l ole Vee sitting by a blue lagoon, "pass my drugs" and a big doctor in white says, "immediately Mrs." "Call me Vee," I'd say. *Babes approaches the bed. Vee casually to Babes without shock.* Take that book off!

Babes Why was you kissing Ga-Ga, Mam?

Vee He's my son, isn't he, a mother's got to teach her son!

Babes *Sings sneakily.* Do you ken John Peel
With his something made of steel
And his something made of rubber
And he stuck it up his mother
And his mother said it's nice
So he stuck it up her twice
And she had two twins in the morning.

Vee *Furious.* Who told you that ?

Babes No-one, Mam. *Quickly.* Know that man, the man in Kong's Mam?

Vee *Leaning back.* Yeah, chinese man, nice man, Mr. Kong.

Babes He did.

Vee *Jumping up.* Did he, the little yellow bastard!

Babes And he showed me a picture of a sheep having a lamb.

Vee What you mean? Intercourse!

Babes Is it ?

Vee You won't go there again!

Babes And he said if he could come in here with his axe he'd smash all these pictures, with his axe.

Vee Yeah! That's what they all say. Jealous swines. Gis the fags! *Babes with difficulty stretches over and passes her posy of cigarettes. She drops the book off her head onto the bed. Ga-Ga darts up and snatches it. They fight. Vee beside herself shouts.* Stop it! Stop it! Shut it up! *Grabs the book herself.* One book we got in the whole house, one book. *Hammers the book with her fingers.* Great pictures of the world! One book! Cissie bought it for Ga-Ga! *Ga-Ga and Babes stand reprimanded. Vee stares hard, lights a cigarette. Opens the book at the first page.* Who did this! Uh? Scribbles!

Babes *Looks over.* Me.

Vee What's that ? *Pointing.*

Babes A dog.

Vee And that ?

Babes A horse.

Vee And that

Babes A sheep.

Vee That ?

Babes A anteater.

Vee They all got square heads!

Babes I did it fast.

Vee Fast be buggered! *Turns over a few pages. Changes tone.* Der! Look at that picture.

Babes *Looking.* Why did those savages do those pictures in caves, Mam?

Vee I dun know, get more money for the caves when they moved.

Babes When the men come home from hunting, they can put

their feet up on the stones and watch the pictures, Mam, innit?

Vee Yeah, *Throws down the book.* I've had enough of that. Both of you get out, I'm tired. *She lies down and tucks up. Ga-Ga takes the book and puts it behind the drape.*

Babes *Walks with Ga-Ga in a wedding procession. Holding beneath his arm as man and wife. Ga-Ga is amused. They stop.*

Do you ken John Peel. With his something made of steel.

Vee Shut up your dirty mind ! Out ! *They exit.*

SCENE III

A dark figure dressed entirely in old worn black clothes. A stained white shirt and crumpled black tie. His grey hair is long and dishevelled. His face is pale and intense and unshaven.

Dai Death *With rich, clear solemnity. His dark eyes address an imaginary audience. This man can see a mental audience at any given time.*

The iron smelting metropolis was a dirty straggling town, sprawling up barren mountains like a bundle of filthy rags, spread out in the hope of them going white. Belching furnaces and black table-top hills of rubbish all around.

A half stupefied sense of the mighty energies of man and fire combined, such as we might feel in the presence of some old monster. Some...., how can I put it, some..... some horrible form. A beast of great mystery belching forth fire and flame. Grim, sooty and strong of limb.

Vee Sooty ? What sooty, Dai ? You silly swine.

Dai Death They are the living past at the dying present. They are the rocket shimmering in the first fright of morn'.

Vee You got fan-tastic brains, Dai. When are you going ?
A figure enters through the kitchen door.

Cissie Come top in college as well, he did. Didn't you, Dai? *Sits by the bed.*

Vee Hi, Cissie. *Smiles at her visitor and holds out her hand. Cissie kisses her hand and holds it firmly.*

Dai Death There was one occasion in particular, rigor mortis set in and he passed gently away, performing his motions. Well, by the time they had him in, he must have been there for what, ten hours in the cold. He was stiff, like this. *Demonstrates.* Old Evan Collier from Plantation Street said. "The only way now is to put up a board, a board, see boy. Look! Across his forehead and nail the board to the sides of the coffin. Well, of course it kept his head down, but his legs were sticking up...like this..they didn't like to break his back, church people, see boy, so they nailed a board across his feet. Without the board like, he'd be wobbling up and down. They don't bury people sitting down, not any more they don't. *Cissie releases his hold of Vee and clicks his fingers.*

Vee Don't you start now, love!

Cissie I got it, love! I got it! New life for old. Use it! Exploit it! The great industrial tail stretching back to the first furnaces. Fire right! Red back-drop, Dai emerges. We'll make a packet, Vee, a side show, moving from unemployed village to unemployed town. Why waste Dai's memories, give Dai a new life. Simple Vee, a simple idea. Listen, listen, listen! How many council houses here? Twenty five, thirty thousand? Repeat the same design, get it, Vee! One design, one unit, repeat it, simple! Whoever did the one design must have made millions! Think simple, Vee! Think simple. We could escape this mess, get out mun! We could ride out on Dai's cancer of the past! Dai! Watch Vee! Dai! *Dai Death turns his head slowly to face Cissie.* Oil!

Dai No axle oil, do you think we cared ? Machines failed to operate, so what did we do? Bacon slices in the wheels! We had them going! Pull together, yes pull together!

Cissie Docks!

Dai Docks! Scab labour! Riots! Government intervention!

Vee Canada!

Dai Ben Canada, always grizzly, like a bear, general foreman, steel smelters!

Cissie Rocks!

Dai Black rock! Mountains! Treacherous in winter!

Vee Milk!

Dai National dried milk, out in nineteen forty!

Vee Sex!

Dai What they put coal in, in Cardiff!

Cissie Pornography!

Dai A sign over Schwartz's music shop, dog looking in a funeral, took it down in the depression!

Vee Jelly and cream!

Dai Bogh Sims! Always talking about snow in the mountains of Spain during the civil war. His phlegm froze in mid-air!

Cissie Whistle!

Dai Policeman's whistle, found it in the gutter during the riots in the Rhondda!

Cissie Get it, Vee, new for old! Shall we try him in the club tonight?

Dai Our steel is laced across continents. Every inch across America is made with our sweat, every foot made from blood and toil, every yard...had a tool-shed and pigeon cot with a decent veg' patch.

Babes *Enters and imitates Dai Death.* O' the terrible ironing board! And the big dog is sucking the sweets! Look at the dirty chair! It's covered in coal! *Turns to Vee and Cissie smiling, they giggle.*

Vee Hey Babes, do it again.

Babes O' the sugar on the table! O' the radio is in the air! Ucher Vee he said to the duck! That's like you, Mr. Death. *Dai Death stares at Babes and exits with urgency.*

Vee You can always come, Dai, we run a rescue service in this house! *To Cissie.* Dai would be the best thing about your act! *To Babes.* Go and ask Betty in the doctors' for paradoxadrinal. Quick! She'll know it's for me! Where's Ga-Ga?

Babes In the kitchen doing God, and the God have got two horns and a eye on his head.

Vee Go and tell him to get on with the secret! *She works on her face once more. Babes goes to the kitchen.*

Cissie Well, here I am, your confidante. Speak up. What's the matter with our star, our Maria Callas of Bloomsbury Crescent, holding court in her Sistine council house. *Babes and Ga-Ga peep into room.*

Vee Paradoxadrinal!

Cissie *Waves away the children* Fly away! Children should be seen only to run messages!

Vee Paradoxadrinal! *Babes and Ga-Ga run away giggling holding the Devil board.*

Cissie *Looking out the window.* There you are, you scraggy little life you! *Points outside.* She's a beauty, she is, out there. She and Him told their kids to keep away from me unless they caught a disease that turned them gay. Know what he asked me the other day? He said, when you die, Cissie, do you think you'll fancy Christ? In all seriousness, Vee, out of the mouths of men like fresh appendicitis scars and eyes like battered daps, hmm! Hold my hand, Maria. We are minorities of one, Vee and I. You could say we're a bit crinkled in the soul, but so what!Those bastards will iron out all crinkles.

Vee Any songs, Ciss?

Cissie Today's a poem, Vee, Hegarty.

Vee Doing it in the club?

Cissie They wouldn't understand, Vee, the poetry of violence on their doorstep.

Vee Do it then!

Cissie We can be sure of one thing tonight.
Hegarty will come mouthing,
Out of his Council seat.
Between the white vested men
on the summer porches.

Around like Togas, this senate.
Say nothing, seen it all before.
Acid in the gold hair.
A blade in the lung, tonight.
A problem of custody.
Look at Hegarty direct as a sign out there
No administration informs tenants.
For example, in make up please,or,
re-do scene two,or hold the hammer,
This way to the screaming head. OK.
Police should come, now.
After Hegarty has swatted the dust.
Round the screams, standing, legs astride.
Firm, resolute.
He grabs the hollow slot between the stink.
OK! OK! He goes again. Lemme sort this out..
I'm a Hegarty.

Vee I like that one, Ciss.

Cissie You're a wonderful liar, Vee. *Peeps out.* It's roasting out there today, in the crag heap. You're up to your knees in soft tarmac. I hate the place, I do. An' I love it. Even when it's sunny, shows up all the skid marks. It's like a torch shining down a rat's vest. They'll put a hook into you, these people, Vee, and pick out what little excitement you've got and pin it up to dry in a mental ward. *Pauses.* I'm getting low. I'll start again. *Walks to door and re-enters.* Hiya, love. *A fussy attitude.* How are you love, today. Say ? *Vee laughs. Sits on end of bed. Vee is delighted* Are you ? Nem mind girl, keep fighting. 'Dun let the bastards beat you.Take this morning, now who did I meet, you know, coming out of Kong's shop but Charlie's Angel and I thought, if she's down here like, shopping, way out of her vicinity, right, something's wrong at the Bungalow. So she looks at me, she says, You know, usual cut and thrust, she said, "Vee alright?" "Why?" I said "Oh!" She said, "It's just I heard she was, you know, rushed in again, stomach pumped." "Listen!" I said, "Who's your informer?" To the bone, Vee. Hey! Hey! To the bone! *Vee laughs* She went like this, "someone!" 'Oh' I said, tell the someone that Vee has just won forty thousand on treble chance and is off in a jet and a new pair of knickers to the Caribbean! Her face dropped. 'O yes', I said. "She's out of it. How's the new Bungalow love?" Off she went, the March hare in full pursuit for a secret rendezvous with her informer. *Vee laughs* Duw! Duw! Duw! I'm telling you. Unless you're on your toes around this estate you could be swallowed down in a tide of filth.

Vee Make me laugh again, Ciss, with stories.

Cissie Know what I am, Vee?

Vee A poetry poof?

Cissie No, Vee. I'm a born again devil worshipper.

Vee Uh?

Cissie I'm beginning to see all of it like Colditz or a Japanese terminal unit, an Iron age fortress, a dark city underground of no escape. Black holes. Nancy and Bill Sykes around every crevice.

Vee Cissie mun, you're making bastarding brainy speeches like Dai Death. Talk ordinary, you sound like the Epilogue. *Babes in her beaver lamb, long dress and high heels clumps into the room, busying and tidying.* Get my...did you? *Babes puffs Vee's pillow, adjusts the sheets, sits Cissie down, shines his cigarette holder, straightens the carpet. Cissie and Vee are awe struck.*

Babes Don't worry, mam

Vee Pardon love?

Babes I'm your slave.

Vee Who you been talking to?

Babes No-one.

Vee You been talking to someone!

Babes No, Mam.

Vee *Shouting* You been talking!

Babes No, Mam.

Vee You been talking.

Babes No, Mam.

Vee You been talking!

Babes No, Mam.

Vee *Pauses* What he say?

Babes Who? That man in Kong's? *Puts her hand to her mouth. Leans back.*

Vee What he say, love?

Babes He was lovely.

Vee What he say, Babes?

Babes He say I was my mother's slave.

Vee I'll get that Jap! I'll blow up Kong's I will!

Babes Mam?

Vee Shurrup!

Babes What's a slave, mam?

Cissie Like a nurse, my sweet.

Babes *Goes to Vee pretending.* You feeling O.K., Mrs? Right then, you have this tablet and you'll be better in the night for the club.

Vee What else did he say, Babes?

Babes Do you ken John Peel with his something made of steel.

Vee Get up those stairs, get those clothes off! *Babes hides behind her hands.* Put you hands down. They don't make you disappear! *Babes goes out, hands still over eyes.*

Cissie The revolution has flaws, darling, when you have spies in Grocer shops. We spend so much feeling on being ourselves in this jungle of machine shop boxes, we don't care about the kids.

Vee You bought him the book!

Cissie Come off it, Vee, Ga-Ga? You talking about our Ga-Ga? Vee, that boy has given the world its first low-tech Renaissance.

Vee What's that? uh? *Myfanwy plays again. Vee and Cissie shout together.* Shut up ! *It stops.*

Cissie *Paces the room. Lights a cigarette.* Council house low tech! Renaissance, see it Vee? See it. Watch it, my love, watch it grow. Boom! council house, open to the public. Queen comes, outside on the porch, navy accessories, white floppy hat and net, short cuban heels. *Vee laughs. Ga-Ga appears.* I name this house jewel in the shit. spirit of the slump. May all these little valley hill-billies with stoat noses and big hats and hoofed feet live in peace with her, and by Royal charter, we have acquired six big welsh homicidal maniacs, with red hair and slit eyes and five scars apiece, studs in the boots and tatoos depicting prostitutes (male of course) to guard her night and day. To the Welsh low-tech Renaissance genius of his day, Ga-Ga, who passed so quickly over the life of Wales, and his mother who got an 'O' level in clapping for the deaf. *Clap, clap, clap.* Haven't you, Vee ? Who thinks her son is not totally deaf, but nothing wrong with him, they gets the Gold Hair-lip Award. *Vee laughs. Cissie runs to Ga-Ga and puts his arm around him in honoured soldier style.* Wear it with pride, my boy! O yes, with pride! Away! Away! Next week, Vee, I'm buying a baby grand and a couple of Beethoven sheets for Babes. Babes! *Babes enters with a saucepan on her head. Cissie and Vee stare in shock.*

Vee What you doing with that on for?

Babes I can't get it off, Mam.

Cissie Leave it Vee, it could be a new hay-fever helmet.

Vee You soft cow. *Takes her to the bed.*

Cissie Sit down, Babes. Listen to this, Babes. Piano, Babes in concert. *Cissie pretends to play, Babes copies.* C'mon ! Come on! Come on ! O yes ! There you are, Vee ! Hideous films presents "If she can make music on the bed, God knows what she can do with a real piano." *Stops Babes.* Get out! Get out! Irene Handle, Vee! Unemployment has taken away my job description, and left me being Richard the Third, making florid speeches into a filthy bush, a roaring boy, Vee, with no political depth. Oh no! Useless I am, love. I'm showing off, I feel a tumour coming on. I'm going. *Walks to window.*

Vee Don't go, Ciss. Day will be a maniac when he comes, with those dullsy batsy eyes. He thinks he's an Irishman when he's drunk. He came home yesterday with welder's goggles on. He said he was 'Itler.

Cissie See you both in self help tonight, Vee. Both with your Duracell smiles. *Walks to the door.*

Vee Don't go, Ciss...Ciss?

Cissie I'll go before the kids come from school. They are all trained to stone me. *Salutes.* Ugliness, ugliness, beauty before bread!

Vee Cissie mun, come back you poof! *Cissie runs back in in panic. Freezes, watching the front door. Turns head to listen.* What?

Cissie *A loud whisper.* I'll be man-handled by a chauvinist in a minute.

Vee Uh?

Cissie Day is coming, drunk, carrying packages and a chandelier. *Raises his finger for silence in an effort to judge which entrance Day will enter. Noise at front door. Cissie exits by the kitchen door.*

Day *Shuffles in, swaying, bent double by weight of packages. Points and smiles at Vee.* I don't care what you say but to me they're fantastic. Ssh! *Puts down the packages, sways. Empties one* *parcel and reveals a large cut-glass chandelier. Holds it over Vee.*

Vee Look at you! One minute you're burning this place down like a box of Swan, the next minute it's a palace.

Day Sugar plus,hey hey! *Admires the chandelier. Flops onto the floor on his back, his arms and legs beat the air like an upturned beetle.*

Vee Babes! Babes! Get the sugar, Babes! *Babes and Ga-Ga enter. See Day on floor and exit.* Sugar! Sugar! Quick! *Enter Babes and Ga-Ga carrying a glass of water and two pound bag of sugar. Ga-ga holds up Day's head. Babes pours in the contents. Vee watches.* So you got the money off the tax man then!

Day *Between mouthfuls and delirious.* Nod a tax-man, sossul security clerk.

Vee So you finished the hobble then? So you finished the bar and optics in his house?

Day *Nods. Sees Babes' helmet.* What you got the hat on for?

Vee She can't get it off, the cow! *Day quickly slams the saucepan and it falls off. Rolls over and scrambles slowly.* Don't run away, swine face! Got any change from seven hundred pounds?

Day Pity mun, he's only a social security clerk. He gim me the chandelier.

Vee So how much he owe you then?

Day He said he'd report me for working on the side.

Vee Jesus Christ, you sucker. *Day reaches the parcels. Holds his finger up to his lips and hands a parcel to each of the kids.* Where's mine then? *He gives her a parcel. Vee gets out of bed and looks at the children.* Get out! And you, sugar. *Opens her parcel and brings out a tiara*

Day Knock 'em in the club tonight, Vee. *Exits into kitchen.Vee puts it on.*

SCENE IV

The fluorescent light of Kong's is dimmed. The room is in darkness. A long bench is placed facing the audience. On the bench is a microphone. To the stage left, a best-suited Day is slumped behind the bench. Vee is next to him in dramatic evening gown.Cissie is next to Vee, dressed in splendour. Dai Death has his hands tied behind a chair, with a gag around his mouth. Spotlights pick out the strange ensemble. A large cloth sign is stretched behind them, with the words "Do us a turn, self-help entertainment" in large letters. Fairy lights surround the stage. Cissie unties Dai Death.

Dai All the colliers were on a three day week, so we stayed down underground, coming up to the surface on the third day we were met by Dick Sheppard. "Boys" he said, "I've got good news." Connelly said it sounded like a resurrection plan. We never did shopping till the night before, markets were open till ten, eleven o'clock. Lamp-lights, snow, everybody laughing. Not those grim looks they got today, traffic bashing and biffing each other, a packet of broken biscuits was only a penny for God's sake. Happy and content, dead now, of course, all of them. I can picture them all out there now, the men with their hair slashed back, immaculate.

Cissie *Grabs microphone. Jumps up and hand gags Dai Death.* Ladies and gentlemen, Dai Death. *Canned applause. Through the mic in a high pitch, affected tone.* To conquer minor skirmishes, or at least to prevent hot blood from rising, would the people of Shakespeare Crescent sit over there. Good! Next to Eliot and Pound Roads. Right! People from Shelley, hands up, right, sit with Byron Avenue. That's right, darlings. O yes, link arms, that's fine. *A long pause, nods his head, puts down his notes.* You know, we're all in this together. The greatest, and I mean the greatest, council estate on earth. *Pauses.* I remember Donald O'Toole, the great Donald O'Toole, who started self help. He said to me when I was a kid, Jeffery, he said, this is the place for children to grow, this is their Eton and Harrow, their Oxford and Cambridge. I won't have them brung up any other way and if it wasn't for that fantastic and I mean fantastic Pools win Donald O'Toole received, I sincerely believe he'd be here tonight. *Canned applause.* I'm feeling a bit emotional tonight and I'm waffling on, let's see, let's get on with the act. *Opens the book.* By the way, that strange smell is me, I'm wearing 'accident in the valleys' by Max Factor. *Reads from the book.*

Some say I'm gay
I wear a rose and a coloured mouth

That's all, I swear there's nothing else
Like illicit sex and quick bucks
In the crematorium woods.
Yet, accosted I was by burly men
with hot eyes on their fists.
They laughed and screamed at my red,red rose
And slapped my coloured mouth
One had a slippery, shaven head
Amid scenes of Paris on his violent shirt
The other with beads and a safety pinned nose
Wore printed images of Great western trains
On his long and bony chest.

Canned applause. Thank you! Thank you once again. Link arms, darlings. Don't be fright, people of Tennyson, people of Shelley, link and sway. *Sways, turns and nods to Vee.*

Vee *Takes microphone. Sings.* Only make believe, I love you. All together! Only make believe, I do. Wouldn't you, wouldn't I, make believe, for to tell the truth – I do !

Babes *Canned applause. Walks onto the stage in a large evening dress and hat with white gloves. The high heels click and make her walk in a ridiculous, comic fashion. At the side of a flabbergasted Vee.* Look mam... look! Look, mun!

Vee What?

Babes Look!

Vee *Embarrassed.* Uh?

Babes Look, I can go cock eyed!

Vee *Screams.* Get her out! Get here out of here! *Day wakes, stands. Cissie rounds up Babes and the two men take her off like a criminal. Lights dim. Spotlight on Vee. A solitary figure like a lost child.* Do you ever get that feeling, living behind a veil thing. Something awful is going to happen. I had it when they took him away from me, he was dead. No he wasn't, he was just different, that's all, different. With his little red tongue, like a piece of felt. Like a kitten. Different. He didn't have arms, mun! He didn't have legs, mun! *Canned applause.*That's not a song, you silly swines! *Sings* And I'll be there in sunshine and in shadow..
End of Act I

ACT II
SCENE I

Vee is collapsed on the bed with Day lying across her legs. Babes is reading from the bible. Ga-Ga is sitting with his book. The dummy is hanging from the ceiling.

Babes *Hesitates and is nervous.*

The song of solomon
How beautiful are th th y feet
With shoes O
Princess Dor
Tur, the joints of th y thygs are
Like jewels the work of the hands
of a cunning workman
thigh nabul is like a round gob

Let which wanteth not liqur th y
Belly is like a heap of wheat set
about with lilies
thigh two bree-easts are like two
young ro-ess that are twins
thigh neck

Vee *Breaks out of her delirium.* He's rogering my leg! *Turns to Day and cuffs him.* What you doing, uh! What are they all doing?

Day Punishments! *Points to Ga-Ga* He's putting glasses and moustaches on all the faces of his book because I said! He hung that up! *Points to the hanging dummy.* Why can't he do alsatians and country scenes like proper artists, not all this, this Doctor Who stuff ? *Surveys room.*

Vee What she doing, dirty man, you ?

Day From the Bible,Vee.

Vee Yeah, sure rogering my leg. Babes! How many times you done that?

Babes Hundreds.

Vee Come yuh! He touch you down there? He touch you down there ?

Babes Where?

Vee Down there!

Babes Where?

Vee Where you go to the toilet!

Babes Upstairs on the landing.

Vee What?

Babes The lavatory.

Vee Get my barbs! *To Ga-Ga and claps the words.* Get on with the secret, it will be my birthday in a minute! *Babes goes to kitchen. Ga-Ga picks up paint palette and leaves. Vee lights a cigarette and lays back on bed.* Drunken, dirty swine!

Day *Points at ceiling.* Three people right, one is made of gold. One is made of steel. One is made of paper. They melt and burn and get soaked, lie there squashed, you Vee.

Vee What you trying to say?

Day Television show, for couples, all the men have beautiful wives, but I win.

Vee Yeah, about time too.

Day I win a bag of rot and smelly water.

Vee Nutter!

Day Then the camera moves to my wife, she takes the prize. She's a rat. The rat sings.

Vee You're having a coma, boy! You must hate me, ai!

Day Punishments, Vee. Series of punishments. Look!

Vee What!

Day Look, mun, between those two black angels, over a bit, by the face in the clouds with rain coming off. *Points to the ceiling.*

Vee Sun that is! *Pointing.*

Day Open it up and there's a room full of Chinese carpets, beautiful tele, twenty feet wide, and chandeliers and music playing, and people without shoes on.

Vee In heaven you mean, sugar-face?

Day And on a big chair all white and shining like a electric shocks is a...a...'er!

Vee A what, aher? What's aher?

Day Looks like you!

Vee Get off me, Day, get off me! Stop taunting me, what you trying to do ?

Day *Gets up and rolls to the door.*Dirty, dirty. We don't stand a chance. Dirty, dirty.

Vee Yeah, stay upstairs, get out of it!

Day Dirty! Dirty! Dirty! *Beats walls and exits, banging continues.* Dirty! Dirty! *Bang! bang!*

Vee Drama club of Great Britain! *Myfanwy plays. Stands on bed and hammers wall. Myfanwy ceases. She clouts figure behind drape. Babes peeps out of door with bottle and water. Ga-Ga emerges from drape with palette. Vee points to dummy.* Get rid of that! *Babes turns off light switch with her nose. Ga-Ga switches on a torch. Babes takes tablets and water to Vee and sits on bed. Vee swallows a few and lies back. Ga-Ga gives the torch to Babes, and lies down behind Vee.* Tickle my back! *With claps.*Tickle my back ! *Ga-ga sticks his foot onto Babes' lap to be tickled, so does Vee.*

Babes *Tries to deal with feet and torch.* Tell me about your brothers and sisters when they were small, Vee.

Vee Hey, come off it, Vee be buggered. *Laughs.* Der, it was marvellous, play all the time on the chapel railings. We were always in chapel, Bandervope, we loved it, ai!

Babes What's Bandervope?

Vee I don't know, it's welsh, means 'all the children come to play'. And every night, my father'd have the boxing gloves. He worshipped me, I was the youngest. I'd box all my sisters and they'd all fall down when I hit them.

Babes You a good fighter, Mam?

Vee Yeah. My father would hammer them if they didn't stay down. He walked all the way from Ireland, pushing a barrow with fourteen kids in it. Talk about a hard life. We had a cat called Dai, who walked about like this, poor dab. *Twists her neck* He worshipped me, my father. Used to buy me white dresses all the time for communion in Our Lady of Saint Peter.

Babes You were Catholic, Mam?

Vee No-one cared when I was small, go to any church. *Pauses, turns to Babes.* I'll get you all christened before Christmas.

Babes What is christened?

Vee Means you can go to heaven.

Babes Can't I go now?

Vee Nu! Wait till Christmas! Feel my heart, Babes! Like bombs dropping. Boom! Boom! Boom! Get another barb.

Babes *Reaches for the tube and hides them.* Tell me about the ghost first, Mam.

Vee That's thirty times this week! *Breathes heavily.* Lying in bed in Adam and Eve Court, woman comes through the wall, dressed in white. Long hair, said nothing, big hand comes out of the wall. Voice said 'Five to live' that's all!

Babes Anyone else see it?

Vee Nu!

Babes How did the voice go?

Vee 'Five to live!' *Cuffs Babes* Shut up, Babes, you're driving me scatty. *Snatches tablets and swallows some.* Keep tickling to a thousand.

Babes I've done five hundred.

Vee Liar! You've only done Thirty! I wish to God I'd gone with her.

Babes Who?

Vee The ghost!

Babes Where, Mam?

Vee What?

Babes A ghost!

Vee Where? *Cuffs Babes again.* I think you got sugar, like him! You won't go to heaven if you act stupid!

Babes Mam?

Vee What?

Babes Where was Jesus born?

Vee Egypt.

Babes Inaninn?

Vee Inaninn.. no..... in a inn, stupid.

Babes A inn?

Vee Pub.

Babes What's it called?

Vee I don't know, The Three Camels, I think.*Drunkenly leans to Babes.* On Hebrew Street. I wish I had normal kids who play the piano.

Babes *With torch moves ghostly round room.* Five to live... eeee.... Five to live. *On mantlepiece picks up mouth organ.* Hee-haw, hee-haw.

Vee Give it to me! Is the deaf nut sleeping? He's not tickling!

Babes *Checks sleeping Ga-ga. Through the mouth organ.* Are-you-sleeping ? Are-you-sleeping ?Mam! Let's play messages.

Vee Go on then, Babes.

Babes I went on a message and got some eggs.

Vee I went... and got... eggs and fags.

Babes I went on a message and got eggs and fags and drugs.

Vee I...on.. a...got eggs and fags, drugs and insulin.

Babes I went on a message and got eggs and um bread? Um insulin. *Shakes Vee* You now, Mam!

Vee I went and fags, eggs, a dress. *Shakes head, calls Babes with her finger and catches her by the throat.* Eggs! Cheese! Chips ! Drugs! and Tommy bloody Cooper, you silly swine. Get to bed, put the torch off! *Babes sits on floor. Thump, thump, thump from upstairs.*

SCENE II

The stage is darkening. The lights of Kong's fade in brightness. Silence. Vee is delirious.

Vee *Sits upright.* What's that ? *A figure in the darkness, Babes, stands at the base of the bed, carrying an imaginary bundle. Vee tidies herself.* Oh. Hello, love. Oh. You brought the baby then.

Well, well, that's nice. *Babes holds out the bundle to Vee. Vee clasps it, and quickly hugs it. She rocks back and forth.* Thank you love. Der. He's never ever grizzled once in his life. He's not a grizzly child, anyway. Are you ? He's eighteen now. I'm saying a lie. Nineteen, he is. Aren't you ? *Looks up.* Oh no. No..No..not this time. He's staying with me, he is. Sorry love, he's staying. Staying with me, he is. Taught me a lot he did. Didn't you? He's different, mun. You know that. So you'd better go then, this one's staying ! Staying here he is, with his Mammy. We'll show them on this lousy estate. *Babes sits on the floor. Vee sings.* And I'll be there... in sunshine...and in shadow... *She sobs.* O god. Everybody must think me stupid, ai. Where's the baby's cot? *Searches around. Finds the bucket.* O ! There's the cot by there. *Puts the baby in the bucket, swings it gently.* Where've you been, mun ? Where'd they take you ? *She places the bucket on her head.* Mammy ! Oh God. Mammy ! Oh God. *Silence.*

Babes *Blows the mouth organ like the sound of Mammy, Mammy mun stop it.* Mammy, mun, stop it. *Blows Mammy.* You know Sparky, Mammy. Does the piano really talk, Mammy? *She lies down.*

A ray of sunlight breaks into the room, increases the intensity. The lights of Kong's take on their familiar harsh fluorescent glare.

Ga-Ga rises walks around bed and checks behind the drape. Looks at shaft of light and moves curtain to let more in. He sees his mother with bucket still firmly on her head. He taps the bucket and makes a grunt. Taps twice, makes two grunts. He feels her cold hands gripping the bucket sides. He hits the bucket hard. His legs shake, he moans, a high pitch moan and runs from the room. Long pause. He runs back, panic stricken and wakes Babes. Mimes a dead body and points upstairs. Points at his mother. Babes taps the bucket, no response. She runs upstairs Long pause. Ga-Ga stands shaking. Babes re-enters, hands together like a nervous bridesmaid. Breathes deeply and changes her attitude to that of a nurse. Walks, now in control of the situation. Points to ceiling.

Babes Now then, he don't need sugar again! *Reflects.* We haven't got sugar, anyhow. We got bread. *Imitation of her mother.*There's no sugar to be found anywhere in this bloody hell hole of a house! I was thinking when I was at Kong's, we usually have sugar. I saw barley sugar and we should have had it. *Back to real Babes.* Silly! No sugar in the house. We could mix pop and sherbet. We haven't got pop in the house. *Thinks and points upstairs.*There's sugar in his box. Empty the sugar from the injections, innit! He don't need sugar. *Looks at Ga-Ga who is shaking. The nurse again.* Right, my boy! *Walks to Ga-Ga goes beneath the bed and takes out radio. Presses and increases volume. Puts the radio to Ga-Ga's ear and watches the high pitch have some effect. Ga-Ga sits holding the radio. As the words blast out, taps bucket and waits for an answer*

Radio Voice "..and what of these poisons, a dark cellar lay gloom, to put an end to the bat's lust or the serpents fanged ascent, wind and fire carve the old beast with distinguished form, devils of the old order march in silhouette on the fire, the fire's light failing to build flesh or form to horned gods, speak, unravel make the snows melt, from what pinnacle does this earth stab the deep sky, to make it speak, and tell of the mysteries unbounded in the one sling of existence."

Babes *Switching it off* Right then. Better ? *Looks at the bucket* Right then, you now. *Rounds the bed, walks to the drape and proceeds to reveal the birthday secret. The large painting is revealed, a Renaissance mother and child. The mother wears a tiara.* The secret, Mam, look. *Ga-Ga grunts to Babes.* Yes, the secret, you know, don't you. *She sits next to Ga-Ga on the bed and puts her arm around him.* Have you heard this one, love ? *Sings* Do you ken John Peel with his something made of steel. And his something made of rubber and he stuck it up his mother and his mother said it's nice so he stuck it up her twice and she had two twins in the morning.

In Shadow

The set is in darkness. Breaking the silence is a hammering on the front door. The door is pushed wide open. Light from a match appears. Candles are lit, and then held high, Stack and Bernie are recognisable. They have carried in paint and brushes and a can of petrol.

Bernie Jesus wept, Jees-zuz wept. *He walks around nervously with a look of amazement and fear.*

Stack Bernie.

Bernie Yeah?

Stack You'll be weeping now, my friend. Gareth! *Stack lights more candles.* Put these around, Bernie. Gareth! *Gareth appears* *carrying steps and a bag of tools. A boy of sixteen, with hearing aids, the flex dangles each side of his neck. We recognise him as Ga-Ga. He wears a white painter's overall.*

Bernie Mr.Stack, it's like those dracula-wolfman films. *Laughs nervously.*

Stack People don't realize, Bernie. *Gives the candles to Gareth.* Put them in the kitchen, kid. *Gareth goes.*He knows where to go look. *Points to Gareth, exiting.*

Bernie *Stops Gareth.* Are you tuned in?*Gareth adjusts a lump on his chest, nods. Bernie grabs Ga-Ga's neck, violently re-adjusts the lump on his chest and shouts into it.* Ever heard of the Mary Celeste ? *Gareth holds his ears in pain.*

Stack Bernie, come here ! *Gareth exits.* Closer, Bernie. *He grabs Bernie's cheeks with his fingers.* Day one, Bernie, day one, we take down all the existing hardboard, plasterboard panels, top to bottom, and we burn them, Bernie, outside, Bernie, day one, Bernie. We plaster and paint, fix in new panels, we paint white, that's why we got all white paint, Bernie, fumigate with Magicote. *Leaves his hand relax* Move, Bernie. Move. People don't realize, Bernie, right and wrong. They get carried away.

Bernie *Tries to interpret Stack's mood.* I was reading the paper today, you know, about er, Elvis Presley's ex-wife, she got a lot of money, you know, the thing is like, should she work?There you are, see, it's got you thinking.

Stack Whole world, Bernie, needs adjusting. Like a cog, move it, in the right direction. Bernie.

Bernie Oi. Oi. Oppression. Oi. Oi. Oppression. Like the young kids feel, Stacky. It's in the band. Oppression.

Stack Flies on shit, Bernie. Move. Day one. Move. *Reaches down and pulls a hammer and a crowbar out of his bag. Gives Bernie the crowbar. Walks to the mantlepiece, taps the hammer on the hollow panels.*Take it.

Bernie Day one. Stacky. This is day one.

Stack taps around the breast. Bernie loosens with the crowbar. One panel is loosened from the base. Gets the steps. Hey. Day one. Hey. *Loosens the top, a panel is torn. Stack and Bernie hold the panel.*

Stack Through the back door.

Bernie *Stands his ground* How many things you taken down, Stacky ?

Stack Everything Bernie, houses, big ships, institutes, royalty.

Bernie Everywhere, Stacky ?

Stack Luton, Birmingham, Isle of Man.Paris, Russia, America.

Bernie Just one thing. Mr.Stack. What you doing here ?

Stack There's a lot for me to do here, in the valleys. Stack's Law, my friend.

Bernie *Reverses, they carry out the panel and half-exit.* I feel sick, Stacky, after all that booze.

Stack Gareth ! Is it paper or board ? Paint it, if it's paper.
Exit. Gareth enters, looks around. Enter Babes. They look at each other. Stack watches from the doorway.

Babes I'm having a baby, *smoothes her swollen stomach* We're all looking for the father now. They don't know who he is. For all they know it could be a black baby. Mammy said I used to be black but she dyed me different colours to go with her clothes. *Looks in carrier.* I've got a nice banana sandwich in here. But it's gone a bit brown. *Hands Gareth the sandwich.* I'm staying with Mr. and Mrs. McCormac in Galsworthy Avenue. They want to foster me, they wears wigs to look younger. I don't know, I've got such a lot to do. Never ending, ai. I'm going, now then. Ta ra. *Walks to the door.* Are you still deaf ? *Gareth shakes head.* O. I thought you was. What you wearing those for then? *Fingers her ears.* So long, love.
Exits

Stack *Against the background of reflected fire in the kitchen* People don't realise, Gareth. But I realise, for a long time I've realised. – Hey. You're still a painter, my friend. *Beckons Gareth with a nod of his head. Gareth walks hesitantly forward. He clenches his fists aggressively.* There's no heroes, boy. Only winners on the day. *Resumes his tacking of panels.*

Bernie *Excited* Crowds are coming back outside, Stacky.

Stack Crowbar it all, Bernie. Move. Day one.

Bernie Lemme take it. Hey. Hey. Day one. Luton. Birmingham. Russia. Isle of Man. Panama. Swedish. Jellicoat. *Exits with a painted panel.*

Stack *Gathers bedsheets into a bundle. Bernie appears and Stack dumps the bundle into his arms.* Burn it. *Bernie carries out the bundle.* Haunted on selfishness. Bernie, the cogs are out of line. *He taps the ceiling with a stick.* People don't realize. Hey. Come here. *Gareth walks to Stack. Stack adjusts the lump on his chest. Holds him behind the neck, close to his own face, takes out his pipe.* I've said and said. Day one. You'll do me good, if you do your work. Shift. *Gareth holds his ear in pain.* Paint it white, paint it flat white, don't come clever, this is the real world, Sonny and I'm Mister Stack, and you remember that good ! *Gareth exits. Stack taps the base of another panel. Levers it with the crow-bar. The panel snaps.*

Bernie *Enters singing* Day one. D..a..a..ay wo-en-en. *Grabs an end, rocking his body in dance.*

Stack Take it, Bernie, take it. *Bernie exits dragging the panel. The fire booms, blaze shimmering.* Haunted on selfishness. *He taps the ceiling.*

Bernie I was reading in the paper, about what goes on behind the scenes in Coronation Street. Der! I can tell you.

Stack Burn it. Paper this is. Paint it. *Bernie exits. Stack climbs down, looks towards the front door.* What you want, red lips ?

Cissie *Enters.* Going a bit far, darling. Muscle brain tactics, don't you think? I've seen everything now, my god. Who are you with then ?

Stack *Walks slowly over.* Who am I with ? I'm only stopping the tide of filth spreading. That's who I'm with, sweetheart.

Cissie Bloody head-banger you look. You stink of booze.

Stack *Leans close* Don't tell me, lovely boy, that nothing went on here, don't tell me that these horned beasts with animal legs, naked women in water aren't some kind of meeting place. But I'll tell you, unless you haven't got two eyes in your head and a brain on your shoulder. People don't realise that with angels and devils and stark naked men there's not nothing going on. Why the deaths, lovely boy ? Go on, answer. I know everything. Suffering on account of all these. Children put in care. It was a meeting place right enough, for movements in evil. Yes, evil. Get out or I'll put you out.

Cissie It's exactly like your illiterate life, isn't it. Those are pictures and images that are famous. Those, for your ignorant information, used to be things that were always done. O yes, but you wouldn't know that, you've spent most of your illiterate life chopping things down.

Stack Ignorant, is it ? *Smacks Cissie's face curtly.* That's how I hit women, because you're not a man. And you know and I know, you were here. Devil worship, wasn't it, lady ? Devil worship. *Grasps Cissie's head with both hands and pulls him across the room.*

Cissie Get off me, you butcher. You bloody butcher. Get off, you sick bastard.

Stack Sick? Sick. Me? Bernie! *Bernie appears* Bernie, quick. We'll do what we did in Luton and Birmingham and Cairo and Warsaw.

Bernie *Half-nelson on Cissie* Ai, Birmingham. Isle of Man. Hey. Hey.

Stack Get him on the bed. Quick, Bernie, in the red mouth for Red Lips. *All three roll struggling onto the mattress.*

Bernie Hey, like in America, Luton, Stacky.

Stack Little adjustments, my friend. People don't realize.

Bernie I'm with you, Stacky.

Stack O yes, Bernie. I'll take you with me when I go.

Bernie Incredible, Stacky.

Stack We'll have the lady's slacks off, Bernie. *Pulls at Cissie's trousers. Cissie is screaming.* Get a clean candle, Bernie. *Bernie fetches a candle.* Hold him, Bernie my friend. *Holds candle up to*

Cissie's face. A little something for you, sweetheart. *He inserts the candle into Cissie.* Give him a little kiss, Bernie. *Cissie falls away. Bernie and Stack laugh. Cissie struggles to his feet, trousers around his ankles. Runs out of back door weeping bitterly.*

Bernie Fantastic. If you...like...go away on salvage again, Stacky. Can I come ? You know like, when I finished community service.

Stack Trust, Bernie. You have to take it on yourself to right the wrongs. Otherwise, Bernie, we'll be up to our necks in a swamp of nutters, perverts, cranks. All out of cog. Biggest estate in the world, this, Bernie, and it needs checking over, dusting in all the hidden cracks, make it clean again, Bernie. Make it function together.

Bernie I'll work for you, Mr.Stack. And after we done the estate, we'll go around again to Germany and America like you done, train Gareth as well.

Stack Bernie, he's being trained now. Day one, Bernie, it's only day one, get Gareth in here. Paint the ceiling. Only paper up there. White, pure white. *Bernie walks to the kitchen door.* Bernie. Fuel the fire with this rotting furniture and say nothing about the queer.

Bernie Right on, Stacky. *Calls to Gareth.* In here now.
Stack collects bit of furniture and follows Bernie out. The fire roars fiercely as Gareth enters with brushes and paint tins. Places them down at the door. Bernie carries steps over to the door, undoes the tin tops with Gareth's stick. Stirs the paint. Both stir the white paint.

Bernie *Singing* Purification, that's the name of the game. In each generation, we play it the same. Purification. *Fades out* Oi, you missed the scrap. In here.

Gareth Who ?

Bernie Say nothing's the best. Li'l secret, 'tween me and Mr.Stack.

Sings again. The fire roars, lights in the room fade. The red light occupies the doorway like a furnace door. Bernie and Gareth stand as dark silhouettes. Dai enters talking to himself and gesticulating. Bernie and Gareth look. Dai addresses his imaginary audience.

Dai What we had see. What we had was power. Raging in the mouth of hell. Men dropping like rain. Children dying in rags. It was the first of the big heaves forward.
Stack appears in doorway and watches the performance. Raises his hand to bar Bernie from moving. He walks slowly to the back of Dai Death.

Dai The place was rich in materials, and of course as you know, the South Wales coalfield was shaped in a 'w' like that. Those were great, great days.
Stack towers behind Dai Death, his arm raised holding a crowbar. The fire roars.

In Sunshine and In Shadow, 1985. Theresa Hennessey, Di Botcher, Phil Babot. Photo: Brian Tarr

Vee's bed, 1993. Sharon Morgan, Helen Gwyn.

Photo: Brian Tarr

THE REDEMPTION SONG

The Redemption Song was first performed by The Made in Wales Stage Company as part of the Write On 87! Festival at the Sherman Theatre, Cardiff with the following cast.

Characters

MICK	Lawrence Evans
BOB	Paul Garnault
BO-BO	Dorien Thomas
BUNNY	Nick Dowsett

Directed by Gilly Adams

The warehouse room is a tip, runs of torn wallpaper, a work bench, saws, hammers and a vice. Broken curtains on a barred window give a homely effect. The floor is littered with woodshaves. There is also a cot, a rocker and a small Welsh dresser, all in fresh pinewood. A large crate lies at the back of the room. It is padlocked. Mick is rolling a joint.

Bob We're in the money, we're in the money! Da da, da dee dee da da dee dee da dar. We've got the patent, we've got the patent.

Mick We're going to make some big money and get out of here. Bob, get this. I move to the door. I dress exactly like this, a little dirty, dirty hair. She say "Dirty bastard, what you want?' I say, "Can I see the kids ?" She says, "Piss off, Dwarfy!"

Bob You got the roller outside, yeah ?

Mick Nu! Not yet. I says, "Please, can I see the kids?" She say, "Oh no, not again, out!" I give her five grand, smack, fresh. She looks stupid, right? I says, "See you next week. I'll give ten grand to the kids. You thought you married an arsehole? But this arsehole, is a genius. Number one." Then I whistle for the roller, *lights up, drawing in* One-half pound of Lebanese is the difference, between, First Avenue snake dance, gripe shit. And the big world up there, *points up, eyes close* One little baby of a dream and you float up there like a god looking down on all the crap, and I'm in that heaven-haven. *touches his lips and kisses the joint* Kisses Maloney, kisses Mickey Maloney, that's his name.

Bob Jesus walked in a hotel carrying nails. Put me up for the night, Butt? I'm so unlucky with women, if I fell into a barrow of nipples, I'd come out sucking my thumb. I'd buy a horse.

Mick Remember Bob, neck and the head of a swan.

Bob Into the four ducks protecting the sides.

Mick Into the kid sits on the Gingerbread man.

Bob Rocks on snails.

Mick Back is an elephant.

Bob And we've got the world by the curlies.

Mick This is the one, just one, wait till the next. Everything a kid wants, go-karts into ships, everything within two feet of his arms. This is the one. It goes in the crate. Nobody sees it.

Bob Get your drawings back from Swansea?

Mick In the box, stamped. Numbered.

Bob reaches for the draw off Mick. Mick rolls another one from his wallet. Bob goes to the crate, dancing silently.

Bob It's locked.

Mick Yeah.

Bob We haven't varnished it.

Mick Fuck it.

Bob Where's the key?

Mick Round my neck, for keeps. I was going to be a priest once and Barbara came in. She used to be a Hell's Angel, next flat, cuts here, cuts down there. I wouldn't let her sit on the chair of God. No kid now. I'd sit erect at the table, polite, and talk to the furniture.

Mick Bo-Bo'll get a mouthful off the Angels. Shitty place anyway. Full of rats and lice.

Bob The rats were polite, mun. "Hallo Bob", they'd say, "gor any filth on you?". *silence* Bo-Bo took my record player, you know the one, the plate. I used to spin it on my finger and put my buck tooth on it. *demonstrates*

Mick looks at the door. Two men in dark clothes appear. One of them has a trilby cocked down over his eyes. The other carries a shotgun

Mick Hallo Bo-Bo. Hallo Bunny. I didn't hear you breaking the door down.

Bo-Bo Where's the toy, creep ?

Mick Gone.

Bo-Bo Get it then.

Mick It's in Swansea. In the office.

Bo-Bo Tell you what, get the toy from Swansea. I'll give you four hours, kid, or so help me I'll kill you. I'll do it myself. I'll kill you, right? You'll be dead.

Mick Get stuffed, Bo-Bo. My brain, my thing, and his.

Bob cringes. Bunny goes to Bob, cocks both triggers.

Bunny Dead. Oh. You're dead, beauty. You're out of it.

Bob is rolled up in a heap on the floor.

Mick This joint keeps going out.

Bob *Terrified* Matches were damp.

Mick Bo-Bo, matches were damp.

Bo-Bo *Arm around Mick's neck* Where's the toy, hardman? *Bunny moves gun closer to Mick's head*

Mick Right. Right. *Falls to knees at side of Bob* Confess you bastard. Confess.

Bob You put it in your mother's iron lung. I saw you do it. Tell 'em. Please. One life we've got, one moment to walk the earth, to touch the sun, smell the autumn leaves. I saw you take it out of your sister's coffin and put it in the lung. Tell 'em, please, for me. Feel clean. Please. Walk again and love the raindrops. Tell 'em.

Bo-Bo *Snatches gun off Bunny to aim at Mick* I gave you the draw, pig's arse. You told me the idea on the draw. Half of what you got is mine. Four hours, pig's arse, you got.
Bunny kicks them both violently. They walk to the door.

Mick *Coughing* Bunny, is it true you were caught, killing the Queen's deer in Windsor safari park ?

Bunny Yes, arse. Why?

Mick Good job.

Bunny Just do the job, kid. And live.
Exit Bunny and Bo-Bo

Bob I saw the land of tables and chairs. *Doubles up laughing* In the iron lung.
They struggle to their feet and Mick laughs his way over to the crate and drapes himself over it

Mick Oh, my little lovely. They all want to ride on you.

Bob Mick.

Mick Yeah?

Bob I've passed over, to the other side.

Mick Listen, mun. Stay cool. We still got this. They can beat me black and blue but I still got this. This.

Bob Gis a ride, Mick.
Bob wraps himself around the base. Both men hang on the crate like the raft of the Medusa. Time passes and they hang there silently.

Bob Mick?

Mick Mm ?

Bob Will Sharon come back, do you think?

Mick Yeah.

Bob Where will you live ?

Mick Ssh. I don't know. Somewhere quiet. *Time passes.* I don't think there will be a reconciliation. But I'll love her to death. I could walk around forever, crying out for her.

Bob I don't think women are worth it.

Mick They get right inside you. And you can't shift the bastards. You just hold on and on, terrified.

Bob Find someone else. You got the money now.

Mick I miss Simp, mun.

Bob Who's Simp ?

Mick A dog in a fucking story in a kid's book.

Bob Remember Barbara ? I was doing my head in one night and I told her I was the force. The force of the whole eternity and if I touched her I could cure her of all little problems on earth and heal up her cuts.

Mick What she say ?

Bob She was doing her head in herself, thinking she was the devil.

Mick Didn't get on then ?

Bob No. Couldn't stand the bastard. It was Star Wars.

Mick What did the rats think ?

Bob She killed them. They turned white. *Time passes.*

Mick *Stands* Hey. In this box. You can't see it, right? Inside, and you can't see it. Believe it, right? Is everything I ever hoped for. Here. Everything. I've done it. I've contained, the force. I don't want anything else. Offer me three houses on Seventh Avenue. A roller, pile of girls, mats, food, nothing. I got it.

Bob Mick ?

Mick Yeah?

Bob If I did the Gingerbread Man.

Mick Yeah?

Bob I got it as well.

Mick Got what?

Bob The force.

Mick Those bastards will be here every hour, checking if we gone to Swansea. Listen. What was the idea?

Bob The toy ?

Mick Right.

Bob Everything is something and something is everything. Multi-dimensional toy.

Mick What did I teach you ?

Bob Um. What it looks like, right ? Appearance, um. What it does right ? Function, um, What it cost. Money.

Mick Last one.

Bob Um, let me think, right. Could it be mass produced?

Mick Right. They are coming to see, eyes. Pass through the door, function. After the money, money. Keep coming till they get it. Mass. I'm a dope head.

Bob You've lost me, Mick.

Mick Pass the problems, out of our hands, into something greater.

Bob Uh? I don't get it now.

Mick Sharon's father is an Indonesian banker. He's got stacks, house in Surrey, house in London.

Bob I don't get it. Why not get Bo-Bo in with a gun. Tell him the rules of the toy. Send him to Sharon's father.

Mick No.

Bob is confused. Silently, with a chisel, he prises open the slats of the crate and peers inside.

Mick Process. Make a toy. Photograph it. Take it to Mothercare. Get a contract for a few grand. Thirty quid a piece rocking horses. Sixteen rockers at thirty quid. Four hundred and eighty quid. Go to a work unit. Have a thousand made up. Get a price. Get delivery. Work unit to Mothercare. We just pick up the cheque.

Bob Remember the rocker at Mothercare ? Four kids fighting over it. Broke it first day.

Mick Shut

Bob Join forces. Fix a point. Which point are you staring at ?

Mick Rip on the curtain.

Bob Which rip ?

Mick Under the fold.

Bob Got it.

Mick Believe in the power. Believe. Believe that there is a force that directs us all.

Bob Oh yes. I feel it. Can you feel it ?

Mick Lose all sense of self and time.

Bob Incredible. I'm floating in space.

Mick Let the force sink inside. Now. Got it. Feel it. Inside. We made the toy before because we believed in the force. It made the multi-dimensional toy. We were just labourers, funnels for the power to come down through. I'm fusing.

Bob And me.

Mick Stare and reach out, bring it here.
Bo-Bo and Bunny enter. See the duo staring.

Bunny *Carries a stag head in his hands, prods Bob with it* I'm not doing it, kid. The animal is doing it. I'm not doing it. Look, the animal's doing it.

Bo-Bo *Grabs Mick by the hair* Swansea, I said. Three hours. *Satisfied with warning, exit.*

Mick Oh god, oh dear.

Bob *Crawls to the crate.* Oh god almighty, mun. Why don't we fuck off ?

Mick They can kill me if they like, I don't care. Even if they maimed me. I still got my joy, in here. I haven't got the bus money to Swansea. Have you ?

Bob Yeah. But I'm not dressed for it.. *Tries to laugh* Phone the the cops, is it ?

Mick They've - been van,

Bob Dullised. Vandullised. The telephones have been vandullised. Give them the patent. They can have my half.

Mick Nu, they don't know what patent is. Bob ?

Bob What ?

Mick I want to live.

Bob And me.

Mick Have you got anyone ?

Bob Girl, you mean ?

Mick Anyone. Family ?

Bob No. I got a brother Mike. He's got a motorbike. He went around the Gower, in a quarter of an hour.

Both find giggling painful

Lights to black. Lights to dim. Lights.

Both singing in the darkness

Will they make it ? Will they take it ? Will they make it ? Will they take it ?

Blackness. Time passes. Mick is in his chair, rolling up. Bo-Bo and Bunny sit opposite. Bunny swings his gun and admires it.

Bo-Bo When did he go ?

Mick About an hour. He's got a lorry driver's tachograph. He'll get a lift fast there and back.

Bunny What's the shit ?

Mick Yours ?

Bo-Bo What's it worth ?

Mick The shit ?

Bo-Bo The toy.

Mick If Swansea like it, fifteen hundred quid. On the nail.

Bo-Bo Anything after ?

Mick Sales. Thirty quid apiece.

Bunny I don't see you with that scrawny piece lately.

Mick That's my wife.

Bo-Bo She pissed off ?

Mick Gone on holiday.

Bunny She's in care. In the hostel. Seen her, and your kids, liar.

Bo-Bo She was drinking with Lance.

Mick Liar.

Bunny Lapping him up, she was. Dirty cow.

Mick She didn't like my pornography collection.

Bunny Boy's don't have that stuff.

Mick I got the best, Bunny. It'll upset you. You. It'll upset your guts.

Bunny rises in temper, goes to stand

Bo-Bo *Holds him back* Stirring the shit, Bunny. You got less than two hours, kid.

Mick Scared Bunny ? Leave him go, Bo-Bo. He's a big boy. But I'll tell you what, a big boy like, ain't seen nothing like I got. Take it, Bun, wank yourself to death. Pubs are shut. Have it. I'm sick of it. Blue films. Two hundred quid's worth. And don't, don't split on me. Don't use the mitts again, O.K. ? In the back room, blue cardboard box, marked eclairs. That's chocolates, Bo-Bo.

Bunny Two miles of Taff. Three times a day. And I'd pour it down your guts, personally. *Walks to the back door. Exits*

Mick Ungrateful bastard. Don't mind me asking, Bo-Bo, but do you believe in Jesus ? Since I saw your ugly mug around town I've been dying to ask you.

Bo-Bo You've had it now, boy.
Bunny screams and enters with a bill hook stuck in his head. Bob follows him with a gun. Bunny rushes in, his hand clutching the point at which the hook entered his head. The loose end waves like a horn. He smashes into furniture blindly, raging.

Mick *takes gun* Out, Out. Or I'll blast you to kingdom come. Get out.
Lights go black. Time passes. Lights rise up slowly. Mick and Bob sit with their backs against the crate. They share the draw.

Bob I was shouting.

Mick Where ?

Bob Glastonbury. Five minutes conversation, fifty pence. Answers to life, thirty pound each.

Mick I'm gone, bushed

Bob And me. *Dim lights to night. Bo-Bo and Bunny stand in front of them.*

Bo-Bo Brilliant. I was foxed throughout. Bloody clever the way you got Bunny inside.

Bunny *Equally posh, stag's head on his head.* Jesus, was I surprised. Speed? Bob just flipped like an acrobat.

Bob Gymnast.

Bunny Gymnast. Oh yes. Swipe! He made it seem so easy. Look, hardly any blood at all. How does he do it?

Bob Practice. Days and weeks at the lathe.

Bo-Bo Anyway, boys, we're off. We've got a lot to tell the gang. You're good, fucking good. *Walk off.*

Bunny Hey, you two, take it easy now.

Bob What did you say, Mick?

Mick Nothing. *Thinking.* You been talking mostly, mun.

Bob What was in that stuff?

Mick Paranormal bush.

Bo-Bo *Reappears at the room door.* Mick? Sorry to disturb you, Mick. But I didn't mean it when I said I wanted half shares in your dream, O.K? And another thing, it wasn't true about Sharon being with Lance. We made it up.

Mick *Mumbles to himself.* I knew you were lying anyway.

Bob What? I'm freezing ai...and starving. Got any chocolate biscuits, Mick?

Mick Yeah.. hold on' Bob boy.. I got a couple behind my yers. *In Mick's head. Lights pass through the window. Like torches, like cars, like the moon. Blue light illuminates the room door and smoke is apparent. Light flickers like an old silent movie.*

Bunny, half beast, half man, posing, in staccato movements, like a Bryan Mills catalogue. Casual with cigarette advertising pyjamas. Surprised and waving to those on a beach. Keep fit. He reverses back into the blue.

Mick See that, Bob? *Nudges him.*

Bob Where?

Mick By the door. In lights. *Bob stares. The lights are red. Bo-Bo appears in a white t-shirt and white trousers, a large XO printed on his shirt. He makes a movement to his mouth continuously.*

Bob XO EXO..EX...OOH. *Bo-Bo signals good, like charades, signals to watch him as he turns. He turns, a large O on his back, turns back, waits.*

Bob OH...EX..O...*Bo-Bo mimes eating.* Got it...Oxo...*Bo-Bo hands are undulating the air like waves.* Gives a meal a *Bo—BO mimes' Come on! Come on!* A beefy taste...

Bo-Bo Gives a meal a beefy taste! *Silence.*

Bob Pity, mun...*Shakes Mick* Pity mun!

Mick *Sings.* Take the world and turn it upside down so that everyone can wear a crown...

Bob Is Bunny dead, Mick? do you think?

Mick *Shakes his head.* If he does right, his gun goes marching on. *Black out for a few moments. Time passes.*

Morning. Lights. Bob is draped from the back of the settee, his arms over the broken back, asleep. Mick is still propped up.

Bob *Wakes up, looks around, stands, walks uneasily to the room, reverses slowly, rubs his eyes.* Mick! See that! *No response. Walks into the room. A water tap is heard. He reappears drinking.* Water, Mick? Water? *Mick stretches his arm while his eyes are closed.Bob walks over to him and gives him the water. He guides it down to Mick's mouth.* I wish it didn't happen, Mick. This is just a new day like...ordinary. Go up the mountain, riding Cleary's horses. Nice day, you know. My head's just..and ugly past..ugly...full of blood.

Mick We did everybody a favour mun! *Staggers up, holding on to the crate and drapes himself on it.* Ther'll be street parties. Jack shit will be the new protector. Long live Jack shit!

Bob Mick. Who's this? *Puts his glass on the crate.* My Frank Spencer imitating John Wayne.

Mick Frank Spencer.

Bob *Laughing* Yeah! No... listen... *Stands, posing like John Wayne.* Chuck away my beret, chuck beret. *Both double up laughing. Poses again. Tough-Spencer -voiced.* OK, Stumpy. I get offa my 'er hoss an' drink a my milk a ...oh..

Mick John Wayne.

Bob Right!

Mick *Points at Bob.* We do the whole human race a favour. They'll give us respect. And Bo-Bo...and Bunny... it's the language they understand. They won't hide behind cops. They'll be a laughing stock to their mob. *Smiles.* Bunny'll have six stitches, O.K.? We keep the Avenues clean. Exterminators. Vermin. When I come up trumps, I get a yacht in Siberia.Two yachts. I don't doubt it. Right. I believe in that crate. And if they cut me up, sonny boy, I come bouncing back in bandages. Because I still got this.*Points to his head.* And I'll put this in Mothercare. In Habitat. Work-units and fifty staff. Focus! Focus! *Both stare. Bob Marley plays their Redemption Song. They sing along together, inspired. Gesticulate.*

Music Why do they kill our prophets
While we stand aside and look
Some people say aside and look
We've got to fulfil dee book...
O'won't you help me sing
Dees songs of freedom
Is all I ever had
Emancipate yourself
From mental slavery
None but ourselves can free our mind OOO!
Have no fear from atomic energy
'Cos none of them can stop the time
O' won't you help me sing
Dees songs of freedom
Is all I ever had
Redemption songs...

Mick is moving now to his mental music, silently, on the spot.

Bob *Arms outstretched, shouting and singing.*
I'm here in America
On a cobbling course
My father sent me
Because I'll show you the broken
Twisted time warp you live in
All will come true...
At the end of time...
Children will walk with Gods
And the injured with the dead..
It's all broken now...
But you'll see the picture in

Twenty ninety nine...
In twenty ninety nine...
Rats will walk in peace
Bunnies in the field
I might have to live all my life
Knowing that I killed a man
Took his human life away..
Me...

Mick Six, seven stitches. We won! Jack the Giant Killers... *Walks to Bob.* Accept it. They put you down. Accept it kid. What you did was with honour. It was meant to be. You fulfilled the meaning. *Sings to Bob, holding Bob's face.*

O' won't you help me sing
Dees songs of freedom
Is all I ever had
Redemption songs...*Stops suddenly.*
Mick and Bob look up to the ceiling, listening.

Mick *Stares at Bob* They're in... *Points up.*

They both walk around on tip-toe listening and looking up. Bob points up. Mick follows a noise with his finger. Bob indicates a noise directly above. Mick indicates to Bob to get down. Shows a climbing action with his fingers. Bob bends. Mick climbs on his back. Bob stretches up. Mick stands on Bob's shoulders, taps Bob's head and points to the glass of water. Bob walks over, collects it and passes it up to Mick. Mick drinks the water and then listens with the empty glass.

Can't reach! *He passes back the glass and hauls himself out of reach. Silence.*

Bob Mick? Mick? Mick? Anything? Mick? *Silence. A large figure of a swim-suited girl advertising holiday snaps is lowered down slowly. Bob undoes it, laughing loudly.* Have you got one up there? *The rope disappears. Figure falls flat. An oil drum is beaten...thump..thump..like war drums...Jaws Film!*

Mick *Slides down with bird's feathers in his hair. American accent.* I dun like it Lootenunt.. I's too quiet..

Bob *Laughing Frank Spencerish.* Is that your hoss outside, ooh! Wella, sumbuddies painted it yella..*Pulls on the rope, jumps up, the rope falls down and Bob falls down laughing.*

Mick Indian...rope..trick.

Bob How did you do it?

Mick I only did a bow.

Bob A bow! *Both laugh, in stitches. They stand, walk over to the settee and sit.*

Mick *Pulls out his wallet and draw. Rolls up, giggles* I done a bow.

Bob Indian brave
Needed shave
Tomahawk slipped
Brave in grave..

Mick *Laughing.* I only done a bow. *Shakes his head.* Hang loose... stay cool.

Bob What's up there?

Mick Nothing... dust.

Bob No windows?

Mick Nu..*Lights, draws in, hands to Bob.*

Bob *Takes it Indian pipe of peace.*
Bumpa Dumpa
Bumpa Dumpa
Bumpa Dumpa *Draws in.*
The poet and the planner
Stood side by side
The poet wrote his poems
The planner did his plans
Can't remember it...
The planner saw destruction... *Hands it back.*
Something about God..

Mick Think Sharon will come back to me?

Bob I don't know.

Mick She got dough... her father's dough.

Bob Indonesian Banker is he?

Mick Ai...as opposed to a Welsh banker. *Silence. Mick draws in.* What she say when you saw her?

Bob When?

Mick When you saw her...in town.

Bob She walked straight past.

Mick Say nothing?

Bob Nothing. To say the God's truth, Mick, she looked thin, teeth were black.

Mick She smiled then?

Bob She was screaming at the kids.

Mick What did she say?

Bob Um?...Fuck off or something..

Mick To the kids?

Bob She's no good, Mick. When you're not around her language is foul. Say you get hundred thousand. World wide, I mean. You know, for the rights, the toy. You could have your pick.

Mick No good, Bob. I want Sharon

Bob Think she's with Lance?

Mick He was lying. Using the old psycho torture. Freaking me out.

Bob Mick?

Mick *Staring forward.* What?

Bob What's the crate doing there?

Mick It's safe.

Bob No but shouldn't we send it off? Swansea... or, wherever you can send it... off?

Mick I don't want to be without it...like a baby. *Turns to Bob.* What do you do when you catch a train... important train?

Bob Catch it.

Mick But don't you always...sort of...feel the ticket in your pocket...make sure it's there?

Bob Yeah, I done that.

Mick Get the crate, Bob. Let's look at it.

Bob *Stands.* She still calls you apathetic.

Mick Among other names. If I go there with the toy, she'd say, 'Hashish heads don't change their spots, toy or no toy.'

Bob *Touching Mick's shoulder.* I'm young, you're young. We're at the prime of our poverty. *Walks to the crate.* They don't know it's inside, Mick. *Turns face lights up.* They don't know. Mark it with another name.

Mick Liquid nitrogen like.

Bob Boot..shoes..um fragile..broken glass. Right Mick, I got it, the rope..up! Put it up there..and us!

Mick Too heavy...too dusty. We got the gun anyway.

Bob Put the gun up.

Mick No, no, Bob. Gun to defend us.

Bob *Cracks up.* Put the gun up. Just the gun. And we all hang around, confident, you know. Fucking gun's up the attic. Bo-Bo and Bunny come in... O.K. Pig's Arse. This is it! – Just smile... *Cracks up.* Secure-in-the-knowledge-of-the-gun-fifteen-feet-out-of-our-reach.

Mick Remember the time you used my razor, old razor blade....

Bob I come down stairs, worse shave I've ever had...

Mick And Sharon pulls the new pack of blades out of her bag... *Laughs at the personal situation humour until they collapse.*

Bob Knock-knock...

Mick Who's there? *Bob whispers and laughs.* Who? *Bob whispers.* Who mun?

Bob *Loud whisper.* Secret police... *Seeing through the curtains.* Mick, you're not going to believe this... *Watching, his head slowly following something.*

Mick *Standing on the settee* What! *a letter comes through the door.*

Bob *Picks it up.* From Sharon.

Mick How do you know? Was that Sharon? *Climbs over.*

Bob *Holds him at the crate.* Don't go out, Mick! Don't go out! It's a trick!

Mick Sharon! Sharon! Sharon! *They struggle and wrestle and the actions turns aggressive until they fall,exhausted. Breathless.* Sharon...Sharon...

Bob Bo-Bo's trick! *Hold around Mick* Cool it...easy....Mick

Mick *Sees the envelope, picks it up, tears it open.* A card with an ape man... *Shows Bob.*

Both *Reading the verse.*

Dear Jack shit
You smoke so much
Because you're guilty
And you're guilty because
You smoke so much
Because you're guilty
And you're guilty because
You smoke so much.

Bob No kisses...turn back.

Mick Hash head on mars...

Bob She came. That's a start.

Mick *Turns the card over, checking.* Rubbed the price off. *Scrutinises.* Does that say "Lance" under those scribbles?

Bob *With his finger, tracing.* No, stupid. Thirty-five pence, 'New-World-Art-Prints'. Hey! It's your Birthday. What would you like?

Mick Sharon and the kids.

Bob *Thinking.* Something second then.

Mick A stand in the British Trade fair.

Bob You'll have all that if you believe in the force.

Mick Hey! If the Universe is us...then I am the Universe....all things are possible.

Bob Same as me. And the Universe is inside us.

Mick We'll get through, see. Just fifty-one per cent to forty-nine. score, thirty-three to thirty-two. We'll come through.

Bob *Shaking with laughter.* And the good die young.

Mick I got half a pound of shit. Today is my earth birthday. I don't care see, Bob. I got stuff, I got the toy...

Bob *Mumble singing.*

Warder threw a party
At the county jail!
Da Da Da Dee Dee...*Blackout. silence. Two red spots of cigarette lights. some moon, car and street*

Bob What do you do then?

Mick Shop-fitting...then pub decor... with a team

Bob Then 'The Incredible Psyche,' the book?

Mick No. I hadn't read it then. Did some hobbling... private jobs. I built a house once and forgot to put in the kitchen. It was in the paper, me scratching my head. Then I read 'The Incredible Psyche' Part one, 'A Lazy Man's Way to Riches', Part Two, 'Authenticity and Simplicity', Part Three, 'You are Providence', Part Four, 'Immortality Begins at Home', Part Five, 'Fulfilling Wishes'.

Bob We're bringing good things to earth.. 'The Incredible Psyche'...O.K! *Silence. The smoke thickens. Bob and Mick cough and hold on to each other.*

Mick *Weeping.* They'll get us...

Bob *Hands him the Kodak girl.* Sharon....Mick..

Mick Sharon... Oh Sharon... *Holds her tight.*

Bob I can't make kids... *Sits in isolation, desolate.*

Mick Give them the toy when they come... *Smoke thickens. Blackness.*

The Redemption Song, 1993. Nick Dowsett, Paul Garnault, Lawrence Evans, Dorien Thomas. Photo: Brian Tarr

The Theatre of the Disturbed Districts

Poor Hugh Thomas. First he had a crazed actor shouting, "This script's brilliant," at him over the telephone, then he had to endure a lengthy rave about the brilliant script he, as director of Made in Wales Stage Company, had given me – *Bull, Rock and Nut*. He handled it with great aplomb.

Let me remind you what it was like in 1982 B.O. (Before Osborne). Only a week before the phone-call, being on a shortlist of two, I had been interviewed by Spectacle Theatre Company for the position of writer in residence. (The other feller got the job -- Frank Vickery.) I remember saying at the interview, given that the population of the South Wales Valleys comprised some 2% of that of the United Kingdom, take all the hundreds of theatre companies, television companies and film companies in Britain and divide by fifty, and this was what our area deserved. And what did we have? Spectacle Theatre Company. (Looking back, this sounds like a put-down. It wasn't meant to be, but I think I've just realised why I didn't get the job.)

My argument was founded on two axioms. Firstly: Theatre is the Art of Society. You probably know the optical illusion that can either be seen as two faces or as a candlestick (unless you're Boyd Clack, who took one look at what I'd drawn and said, "A candlestick kissing itself.") Society is the candlestick, the space between our faces, our interface, and that's what theatre is about. It is the block the theatrician sculpts, it is his paint, his piano.

Incidentally, this refutes the usual argument that theatre is the bastard art in that it is a hotchpotch of all the others: literature, movement, music, visual arts and so on. Theatre is the purest art because its substance – the social interface – is all at once its subject-matter, its working-method and its end-product.

Alan's theatre, of course, is the art of the society my heart most bleeds for : the post-industrial South-East Wales Valleys. The area known in the nineteenth century as the Disturbed Districts. (I can handle that.) But at the time of the interview Alan hadn't happened.

My second axiom was: Theatre is to Society as Language is to the Individual (and I use theatre here to mean all the dramatic media, including television and film). Just as the individual uses language to explore him- or herself, define him- or herself, and then express him- or herself to other individuals, so society uses theatre to explore itself, define itself, and then express itself to other societies. A society without theatre is therefore like an individual without language. And this was how we were. Before Alan.

The last job I'd had before my pompous rhetoric totally destroyed my chances of getting that job with Spectacle Theatre Company had been with Foco Novo at the Roundhouse, under Roland Rees. Roland, being Welsh himself, didn't share the usual London theatre-director's antipathy towards the Welsh accent. So when I asked him what accent he wanted me to play the part in, he said, "Your own."

To my horror I found I couldn't do it. I didn't know what it sounded like. I had no role-models, except for certain television parodies who shall remain nameless, but you know who you are. The Valleys had no voice. I ended up playing the part Cardiff, which London audiences thought was bad Liverpool.

Then Hugh Thomas gave me the script of *Bull, Rock and Nut*. Before I'd finished the first page, I knew. I knew – for a fact – that it was totally unreadable. I got about three pages in and gave up. There was no hurry after all. The second time I only got halfway down page one. When rehearsals were looming horribly large I sat down and thought, "Who do I know from Merthyr ?" and my mate Louis came to mind. So I started reading it again, this time with Bull, Rock and Nut all speaking as Louis. About half an hour later I phoned Hugh and shouted, "This script's brilliant."

Here was the voice I had, in that interview only a week before, been saying we lacked. Here was our theatre – a meta-language for our society. Not a "boyo" to shake a stick at, much as I'd have liked to. This stuff never even looked, for the briefest moment, like coming anywhere near the merest hint of a shadow, of a sniff of a cliche. So this was what I sounded like. And I'm not talking about accent here. What this man, this Alan Osborne, had done was, for the first time ever, to create a dramatic poetry out of our use of language – its music, its rhythms, its momentum, its choice of words, its choice of silences, its imagery, its cultural references, its historical context, in short, our voice. The Theatre of the Disturbed Districts would, quite simply, never be the same again.

Dorien Thomas
1998

Alan Osborne. January 1998, Cardiff.

Photo: LD